"A"

By the same author

"A" 1–12

LOUIS ZUKOFSKY

PARIS REVIEW EDITIONS

Doubleday & Company, Inc., 1967, Garden City, New York

Acknowledgments for appearances from 1931-1959 of parts of the contents of this volume, to:

Poetry (Chicago)
The New Review (Paris)
To, Publishers (Le Beausset, Var)
Faber and Faber (London)
New Directions (Norfolk, Conn.)
Calendar (Prairie City, Ill.)
Cronos (Columbus, Ohio)
Botteghe Oscure (Rome)
Montevallo Review (Montevallo, Ala.)
Beloit Poetry Journal (Beloit, Wis.)
Black Mountain Review (Black Mountain, N. C.)
Return (Provincetown, Mass.)
Origin Press (Kyoto)

Library of Congress Catalog Card Number 67-23819

Printed in the United States of America

First Edition in the United States of America

foreword
"A"

a poem of a life

—and a time. The poem will continue
thru 24 movements, its last words still
to be lived. Bach is a theme all thru
it, the music first heard in 1928
affecting the recurrences or changes
as may be of the story or history.

After 40 years of the writing and still
with it, it is easier to say *here it is*
than explain what seems to me to be clear.
It comes to as I have said elsewhere
(somewhat differently):

*not to fathom time but literally to sound
it as on an instrument and so to hear
again as much of what was and is together,
as one breathes without pointing to it
before and after. The story must exist in
each word or it cannot go on. The words
written down—or even inferred as written
over, crossed out—must live, not seem
merely to glance at a watch.*

L. Z.
2/25/67

A Note

There is a possibility in reading and writing, which knows words as in the world as much the same way that men are, and that each may know that possibility which Herrick defines:

> And when all bodies meet,
> In Lethe to be drowned,
> Then only numbers sweet
> With endless life are crowned.

There is no presumption in the fact that Louis Zukofsky puts two poems of Herrick's together with his own song, "Little wrists," as an instance of *grace* in his comparative anthology, *A Test of Poetry*. One hears in the possibility another has articulated what may thus bring clear one's own, and though there are three hundred years intervening the measure of grace is not variable.

Zukofsky says, one writes one poem all one's life. All that he has written may be felt as indivisible, and all *one*—which word occurs frequently in the text in this sense.

Another word found often is *leaf*, echoing, specifically at times as in the latter part of *"A" 12,* Whitman's *Leaves of Grass*. Despite what seem dissimilarities, they are like men in that both would favor—with Shakespeare as Zukofsky has pro-posed—the "clear physical eye" as against "the erring brain." The experience of one's life as one is given to have it, and as relationships of its nature are found, unfold, then, as *leaves,* finding home in time far past or in the instant now:

The music is in the flower,
Leaf around leaf ranged around the center;
Profuse but clear outer leaf breaking on space,
There is space to step to the central heart:
The music is in the flower,
It is not the sea but hyaline cushions the flower—
Liveforever, everlasting.
The leaves never topple from each other,
Each leaf a buttress flung for the other.

This is taken from *"A" 2,* written in 1928. In *"A" 11,* twenty-two years later:

Honor

His voice in me, the river's turn that finds the
Grace in you, four notes first too full for talk, leaf
Lighting stem, stems bound to the branch that binds the
Tree, and then as from the same root we talk, leaf
Over leaf of his thought, sounding
His happiness: song sounding
The grace that comes from knowing
Things, her love our own showing
Her love in all her honor.

"…His voice in me…" That men do so move, one to one, here grandfather, to father, to son—but that also, as Zukofsky thinks possible, it may be that Shakespeare had read Catullus, and that men who may so read the same text may so *in time* relate. Certainly, as the outset of the work makes clear, Zukofsky *hears* Bach, and after hearing:

> I walked on Easter Sunday,
>> This is my face
>> This is my form.
>> Faces and forms, I would write
>>> you down
>> In a style of leaves growing.

One may well quote Pound, as Zukofsky has, to give measure for such occasion:

> Hast 'ou fashioned so airy a mood
>> To draw up the leave from the root?
>>> . . .
> and the rest as time has cleft it

The title *"A"* itself is what one might call initial, and initiating, evidence of the kind of intelligence Zukofsky has—seeing and hearing words in the world as the specific possibilities they contain. He has said, in fact, that "a case can be made out for the poet giving some of his life to the use of the words *the* and *a:* both of which are weighted with as much epos and historical destiny as one man can perhaps resolve." How much "world" can lie between *the* and *a* is hardly for either *a* or *the* grammarian to decide.

We may speak of *the* as some thing previously noted or recognized, and of *a* as that which has not been thus experienced—but think too that, "from A to Z" may mean something, and that if one looks at an A, it may very possibly become a sawhorse:

Horses: who will do it? out of manes? Words
Will do it, out of manes, out of airs, but

They have no manes, so there are no airs, birds
Of words, from me to them no singing gut.
For they have no eyes, for their legs are wood,
For their stomachs are logs with print on them;
Blood red, red lamps hang from necks or where could
Be necks, two legs stand A, four together M.

Horses and *leaves:*

You keep up to date
On all fours
That canter sometimes
Before boughs that grace trees.
Sparks from hoofs:
There is horse...

So year to year—
Nor do the arts
Ever end.
How can man say
"I am certain"
For certain and uncertain
Do not make certain.
Only forever is previous
And not a horse's forever.
If someone stole off with its body
Be sure that its spirits
Canter forever.
Blacksmith, creator, shapes his shoe
Into substance.

Born in New York's lower east side, Zukofsky's life cannot
have been simple, and the kinds of complexity one realizes do
confront him here are deeply to be considered. In the opening
movements there are bitter terms of death, poverty, war—

"I beg your pardon
I've a—"h" begins the rhyme here,
Shall we now?"

"You misconstrue—uh
Men's rue—eh,
Anyhow!"

The sailors in the carousel
    looking for a place to
        bury—Ricky;
Seaweed, fellow voters, and
    spewn civic sidewalks.

Thus one modernizes
His lute,
Not in one variation after another;
Words form a new city,
Ours is no Mozart's
Magic Flute—
Tho his melody made up for a century
And, we know, from him, a melody resolves
                            to no dullness—
But when we push up the daisies,
The melody! the rest is accessory:

My one voice. My other: is
An objective—rays of the object brought to a focus,
An objective—nature as creator—desire
    for what is objectively perfect
Inextricably the direction of historic and
                        contemporary particulars.

He was first published in *Exile* by Ezra Pound in the twenties.
The poem was "The," which is relevant, and it led subsequently
to his publication in *The Dial* and other magazines of the period. In 1931 he edited an issue of *Poetry* in which he presented

a number of writers, among them Carl Rakosi, Kenneth Rexroth (for whom it was his first publication), William Carlos Williams (whose poem "The Alphabet of the Trees" gained him one of his first awards), and others of like significance. Asked for some tag, whereby to identify the group, Zukofsky used the term "objectivist"—which he once spoke of in conversation as follows:

> I picked the word simply because I had something very simple in mind. You live with the things as they exist and as you sense them and think them. That's the first thing, and that I call *sincerity* in an essay that was printed at the back of that *Poetry* number. Otherwise how sincere your intentions doesn't matter. The rest is, once you do that, you do put them into a shape that, apart from your having lived it, is now on its own, and that's what goes into the world and becomes part of it.

He has been long and quietly about his work, and, in the passage of time, he has written other books which complement it significantly—*All,* the collected short poems in two volumes (1923–1958; 1956–1964) and *Bottom: on Shakespeare* (published in 1963) among them. What he has said of the latter makes a useful focus here. First, despite that it is written in prose, he calls it "a long poem on a theme for the variety of its recurrences." The theme is, "that Shakespeare's text thruout favors the clear physical eye against the erring brain" and "that this theme has historical implications." Second, a "valid skepticism, that, as 'philosophy of history' taking in the (arts and sciences) my book takes exception to all philosophies from Shakespeare's point of view, that is, the physical eye against the erring brain." Third, "a continuation of my work on prosody in my other writings. In this sense my wife's music [her setting of Shakespeare's *Pericles* is the second volume of this work] saves me a lot of words, and she did a note to every syllable of *Pericles*." Finally, it is "a poet's autobiography as involvement of twenty years in a work shows him up, or, as in the case of Shakespeare, his words show him, are his life..."

About *All*, Mr. Zukofsky says: "In a sense *All* is an autobiography: the words are my life...Or to put it in other words, the poet's form is never an imposition of history, but the desirability of making order out of history as it is felt and conceived."

In the title story of *It was*, a collection published in 1961, the story itself having been written twenty years earlier, one finds: "This story was a story of our time. And a writer's attempts not to fathom his time amount but to sounding his mind in it. I did not want to break up my form by pointing to well-known place names and dates in the forty years that I had lived —events familiar to most of us, to some more than myself. I wanted our time to be the story, but like the thought of a place passed by once and recalled altogether: seen again as through a stereoscope blending views a little way apart into a solid—defying touch. I was saying something that had had a sequence, like the knowledge of taking a breath, and hiding it, because one breathes without pointing to it before and after..." "Thanks to the Dictionary," the final piece of this same book, written in 1932, begins:

"A." Quoting the dictionary. Remembering my sawhorses, my little a.'s abbreviated for afternoon, perhaps for years, this afternoon.

Quoting Satie, "born very young in a world already old," he has said of *"A,"* "The idea is much as the brain does err, it will willynilly get down, and sometimes the eye sees—the form in that sense organic, or all of one's life, and this is the life, and for the rest nobody else's business. "It's written in one's time and place, and it refers to other times and places as one grows, whatever way one grows. It takes in books that survive—say, well, like Bach's music it can go down, it can go up, that's the interest of it and all to come through the form of the thing. To hold it together, I don't know—a song?''

From "A" 12:

You remember
The houses where we were born
The first horse pulsed
Until the evening and the morning
Were the first day?

I'll tell you
About my *poetics*—

$$\int \begin{array}{l} \text{music} \\ \text{speech} \end{array}$$

An integral
Lower limit speech
Upper limit . . .

* * *

Time qualifies the fire and spark of it.
I can't improve *that*.
That closed and open sounds saw
       Things,
See somehow everlastingly
Out of the eye of sky.

Poetics. With constancy . . .

* * *

As I love:
My poetics . . .

* * * .

Better a fiddle than geiger?
With either there is so much in 1

And in one:

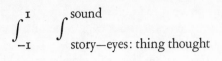

$$\int_{-1}^{1} \int \genfrac{}{}{0pt}{}{\text{sound}}{\text{story—eyes: thing thought}}$$

* * *

Courses tide, and a tide
   brings back folk
   after twenty years,
A cycle a light matter or more,
So my song with an old voice is whole:
Another way of saying
You cannot take out of the circle—what was in it . . .

Thus to *hear,* as he would hear Catullus, in the translation
he has made with his wife—"fact that delights as living hint
and its cues" being "facit delicias libidinesque"—"which is
much more simple in the Latin. It has to do with pleasures
and desires . . ." So *"A"* 9 is an extraordinary reading of Guido
Calvacanti's *Donna mi prega,* the *experience* of valuation, and
of love, with Marx as he stems from Aristotle included—the
form a canzone, which demands that fifty-four of the one
hundred and fifty-four syllables occurring in a strophe be
rhymed, extending to seventy-five lines in all. As Zukofsky
notes, "it's all wound in," which impulse the sonnet form reverses. Here he has composed two distinct canzones—the first,
of value, the second, of love—not a literal translation of Calvacanti but rather an intensive experience of the intimate situation
of his writing, as fact of sounds in the rhythms then relating.

The second canzone repeats, almost verbatim, the rhymes of the first:

(1)
An impulse to actions sings of a semblance
Of things related as equated values,
The measure all use is time congealed labor
In which abstraction things keep no resemblance
To goods created; integrated all hues
Hide their natural use . . .

(2)
An eye to action sees love bear the semblance
Of things, related is equated—values
The measure all use who conceive love, labor
Men see, abstraction they feel, the resemblance
(Part, self-created, integrated) all hues
Show to natural use . . .

To know what men say, one must hear them, and to hear them means moving with the intimate means of their occasion.

* * *

Out of deep need
Four trombones and the organ in the nave
A torch surged—
Timed the theme Bach's name
Dark, larch and ridge, night:
From my body to other bodies
Angels and bastards interchangeably
Who had better sing and tell stories
Before all will be abstracted.

Buffalo, N.Y.   Robert Creeley
April 2, 1967

"A"

1

A
  Round of fiddles playing Bach.
    Come, ye daughters, share my anguish —
  Bare arms, black dresses,
    See Him! Whom?
  Bediamond the passion of our Lord,
    See Him! How?
His legs blue, tendons bleeding,
    O Lamb of God most holy!
Black full dress of the audience.
Dead century, where are your motley
Country people in Leipzig,
Easter,
Matronly flounces, starched, heaving,
Cheeks of the patrons of Leipzig —
"Going to Church? Where's the baby?"
"Ah, there's the Kapellmeister
    in a terrible hurry —
Johann Sebastian, twenty-two
    children!"

  The Passion According to Matthew,
  Composed seventeen twenty-nine,
  Rendered at Carnegie Hall,
  Nineteen twenty-eight,
  Thursday evening, the fifth of April.
  The autos parked, honking.

A German lady there said:
  (*Heart turned to Thee*)
"I, too, was born in Arcadia."

The lights dim, and the brain when the flesh dims.
Hats picked up from under seats.
Galleries darkening.
"Not that exit, Sir!"
Ecdysis: the serpent coming out, molting,
As tho blood stained the floor as the foot stepped,
Bleeding chamfer for shoulder:
"Not that exit!"
"Devil! Which?" —
Blood and desire to graft what you desire,
But no heart left for boys' voices.
Desire longing for perfection.

And as one who under stars
Spits across the sand dunes, and the winds
Blow thru him, the spittle drowning worlds —
I lit a cigarette, and stepped free
Beyond the red light of the exit.

The usher faded thru "Camel" smoke;
The next person seen thru it,
Greasy, solicitous, eyes smiling minutes after,
A tramp's face,
Lips looking out of a beard
Hips looking out of ripped trousers
                          and suddenly
Nothing.
About me, the voices of those who had
                    been at the concert,

Feet stopping everywhere in the streets,
High necks turned for chatter:
"Poor Thomas Hardy he had to go so soon,
He admired so our recessional architecture —
What do you think of our new Sherry-Netherland!"
"Lovely soprano,
Is that her mother? lovely lines,
I admire her very much!"
And those who perused the score at the concert,
Patrons of poetry, business devotees of arts and letters,
                   Cornerstones of waste paper, —
"Such lyric weather" —
Chirping quatrain on quatrain;
And the sonneteers — when I consider
                again and over again —
Immured holluschickies persisting thru polysyllables,
Mongers in mystic accretions;
The stealers of "mélange adultère de tout,"
Down East, Middle West, and West coast flaunters
               of the Classics and of
                     Tradition
(A word to them of great contours) —
Who sang of women raped by horses.

And on one side street near an elevated,
Lamenting,
Foreheads wrinkled with injunctions:
"The Pennsylvania miners are again on the lockout,
We must send relief to the wives and children —
What's your next editorial about, Carat,
We need propaganda, the thing's
               becoming a mass movement."

It was also Passover.

The blood's tide like the music.
A round of fiddles playing
Without effort —
As into the fields and forgetting to die.
The streets smoothed over as fields,
Not even the friction of wheels,
Feet off ground:
As beyond effort —
Music leaving no traces,
Not dying, and leaving no traces.

Not boiling to put pen to paper
Perhaps a few things to remember —

"There are different techniques,
Men write to be read, or spoken,
Or declaimed, or rhapsodized,
And quite differently to be sung";
"I heard him agonizing,
I saw him *inside*";
"Everything which
We really are and never quite live."
Far into (about three) in the morning,
The trainmen wide awake, calling
Station on station, under earth,

> *Cold stone above Thy head.*
> *Weary, broken bodies.*
> *Sleeping: their eyes were full of sleep.*

The next day the reverses
As if the music were only a taunt:
As if it had not kept, flower-cell, liveforever,
        before the eyes, perfecting.

— I thought that was finished:
Existence not even subsistence,
Worm eating the bark of the street tree,
Smoke sooting skyscraper chimneys,
That which looked for substitutes, tired,
Ready to give up the ghost in a cellar —
Remembering love in a taxi:
A country of state roads and automobiles,
But great numbers idle, shiftless, disguised on streets —
The excuse of the experts
'Production exceeds demand so we curtail employment';
And the Wobblies hollering reply,
Yeh, but why don't you give us more than a meal
          to increase the consumption!
And the great Magnus, before his confrères in industry,
Swallow tail, eating a sandwich,
"Road map to the stomach," grinning,
Pointing to a chart, between bites.

"We ran 'em in chain gangs, down in the Argentine,
Executive 's not the word, use *engineer*,
Single handed, ran 'em like soldiers,
Seventy-four yesterday, and could run 'em today,
Been fishin' all Easter
Nothin' like nature for hell-fire!"

Dogs cuddling to lamposts,
Maybe broken forged iron,
        "*Ye lightnings, ye thunders
        In clouds are ye vanished?*

        Open, O fierce flaming pit!"

2

— Clear music —
Not calling you names, says Kay,
Poetry is not made of such things,
Music, itch according to its wonts,
Snapped old catguts of Johann Sebastian,
Society, traduction twice over.

— Kay, in the sea
There with you,
Slugs, cuttlefish,
Ball of imperialism, wave games, nations,
Navies and armaments, drilling,
Old religions —
Epos:
One Greek carrying off at least two wives for his
                                        comfort —
Those epopt caryatids, holding, holding, the
                                        world-cornice.
(Agamemnon). Very much like the sailors.
Lust and lust. Ritornelle.
All! blue trouser seats — each alike a square inch —
      sticking thru portholes,
Laughter, laced blue over torus,
Gibes from the low deck:
"Hi, Ricky!"
(Splash of white pail-wash, scuttling and laughter).
The sea grinds the half-hours,
Each half-hour the bells are heard,

Half-human, half-equestrian, clatter of waves,
Fabulous sea-horses up blind alleys,
Never appeased, desire to break thru the walls
                                of alleyways:
Till the moon, one afternoon,
Launches with sea-whorl,
Opening leaf within leaf floats, green,
On waves: liveforever.
Hyaline cushions it, sun,
In one's own head.

As in Johann Sebastian,
Listen, Kay . . .
The music is in the flower,
Leaf around leaf ranged around the center;
Profuse but clear outer leaf breaking on space,
There is space to step to the central heart:
The music is in the flower,
It is not the sea but hyaline cushions the flower —
Liveforever, everlasting.
The leaves never topple from each other,
Each leaf a buttress flung for the other.

Ankle, like fetlock, at the center leaf —
Looked into the mild orbs of the flower,
Eyes drowned in the mild orbs;
Hair falling over ankle, hair falling over forehead,
What is at my lips,
The flower bears rust lightly,
No air stirs, but the music steeps in the center —
It is not the sea, but what floats over it.

                    Or

I walked on Easter Sunday,
>This is my face
>This is my form.
>Faces and forms, I would write
>>you down
>In a style of leaves growing.

A train crossed the country: (cantata).
A sign behind trees read (blood red as intertwined
>Rose of the Passion)
>>Wrigleys.
Boy and girl with crosses of straw for their nosegays
Impinged upon field as on ocean;
Breath fast as in love's lying close,
Crouched, high — O my God, into the flower!

The double chorus singing,
>*Around Thy tomb here sit we weeping*
For the fun of it,
>*O Saviour blest*
The song out of the voices.

3

At eventide, cool hour
Your dead mouth singing,

Ricky,

Automobiles speed
Past the cemetery,

No meter turns.
Sleep,

With an open gas range
Beneath for a pillow.

The cat, paw brought back
Over her seat, velvet,

Puss — .

"Who smelt gas?"
"— Would I lie!"

"No crossin' bridges,
Rick'—
No bridges, not after midnight!"

"— God's gift to woman!"

Out of memory
A little boy,

It's rai-ai-nin',

Ricky,
Coeur de Lion.

Lion-heart,
A horse bridled —

Trappings rise,
Princelet
Out of history.

Trappings
Rise and surround

Two dark heads,
Dead, straight foreheads,

The beautiful
Almost sexual

Brothers.

I, Arimathaea,
His mirror,
Lights either side —

> *Go,*
> *Beg His corpse*

— Wish I had been broken!

In another world
We will not motor.

Dead mouth
(Cemetery rounded

By a gastank)

The song reaches home
'Here are your dead,

Not yours —
A broken stanchion.

Of leaves,

Lion-heart, my dove,
Pansy over the heart, dicky-bird.'

4

Giant sparkler,
Lights of the river,

(Horses turning)
Tide,

And pier lights
Under a light of the hill,

A lamp on the leaf-green
Lampost seen by the light

Of a truck (a song)
Lanterns swing behind horses,

Their sides gleam
From levels of water —

Wherever we put our hats is our home
Our aged heads are our homes,
Eyes wink to their own phosphorescence,
No feast lights of Venice or The Last Supper light
Our beards' familiars; His
Stars of Deuteronomy are with us,
Always with us,
We had a Speech, our children have
                        evolved a jargon.

We prayed, Open, God, Gate of Psalmody,

That our Psalms may reach but
One shadow of Your light,
That You may see a minute over our waywardness.
Day You granted to Your seed, its promise, Its

> Promise,

Do not turn away Your sun.
Let us rest here,
> lightened
Of our tongues, hands, feet, eyes, ears and hearts.

> Fierce Ark!
> Gold lion stomach
> (Red hair in intaglio)
> Dead loved stones of our Temple walls,
> Ripped up pebble-stones of our tessellation,
> Split cedar chest harboring our Law,
Even the Death has gone out of us — we are void.

> Hear —
> *He calleth for Elias —*
> A clavicembalo!

Deafen us, God, deafen us to their music,
Our own children have passed over to the ostracized,
They assail us —
> 'Religious, snarling monsters' —
And have mouthed a jargon:
> "Rain blows, light, on quiet water
> I watch the rings spread and travel
> Shimaunu-Sān, Samurai,
> When will you come home? —
> Shimaunu-Sān, my clear star.

> To-day I gather all red flowers,

Shed their petals on the paths,
Shimaunu-Sān, in the dawn,
   Red I go to meet him —
      Shimaunu-Sān, my clear star.

To-morrow I tear cherry sprays,
   Wreathe them in my hair and at my
                                 temples,
Shimaunu-Sān will see my head's white
                                 blossoms,
   In the dark run towards me
      Shimaunu-Sān, my clear star.

All turtle-doves have pledged
   To fly and search him:
Shimaunu-Sān, at my little windows
   Each night a tiny candle will be
                              lighted —
      Shimaunu-Sān, my clear star."

— *Yehoash.*

Song's kinship,
The roots we strike.

"Heavier from day to day
Grow my limbs with sap of forests"

"Deep roots hammer lower"

"And to the Sun, I bow.
On the gray mountains,
Where multiply
The stairs of crags, my prayer
Will follow you, still Heir —

Bestower —
Of man and tree and sand,

When your face upon the land
Flames in last redness, allow me of your
light —"

My father's precursors
Set masts in dinghies, chanted the Speech.

"Wider is the ash around the fire"
"Treasures turned to sand"

Yehoash, —
The courses we tide from.

Tree of the Bach family
Compiled by Sebastian himself.
'   Veit Bach, a miller in Wechmar,
Delighted most in his lute
Which he brought to the mill
And played while it was grinding.
A pretty noise the pair must have made,
Teaching him to keep time.
But, apparently, that is how
Music first came into our family!'

A carousel — Flour runs.
Song drifts from the noises.

"My petted birds are dead."

"I will gather a chain
Of marguerites, pluck red anemone,

22

Till of every hostile see
Never a memory remain."

5

An animate still-life — night.
Leaves, autumn.
Thread the middle.

             A cigarette,
Leaf-edge, burning
           obliquely urban,

        the branches of trees air
              comfort.

Kay: The heart has the imagination,
In case of emergency follow the next lunatic.

I: Ask Faust, the reason we're not further along —
Go-ethe, alias MacFadden —
He-er vent Hel-ee-na squat from our sidewalks.

        One's thought

And past the leaf's edge
(Not in the central heart)
Our voices:
    "How? without roots?"
    "I have said *The courses we tide from.*"
    "They are then a light matter?"
    "Let it go at that, they are a light matter."
    "Isn't it more?" "As you say."
    "Your people?" "All people."

"You write a strange speech." "This."

One song
Of many voices:

The words Matthew weeps
(Plaint, clavicembalo) —
    Chorale, the kids in the loft
    (*O love untold*, love lying close);
Or say, words have knees
        water's in them, all joints crack, —
    (New York, tonight, the rat-lofts
            light
            with the light of a trefoil);

Purple clover,
She wore her shoes three years —
    (The soles new as the sunned black
        of her grave-turf);
Speech bewailing a Wall,
Night of economic extinctions
Death's encomium —
    And leaves blowing over and over.

        For I have seen self-taunt
           tracked down in the mirror,
        And besides it, asleep, the face open,
        Edges of no one like it: Everlasting.

And one afternoon: a field,
Two windows spacing a wall,
A heavy bulk move back of
        the windows —

A field behind brick wall, painted
        with gigantic green elves, Wrigleys in
                rubric —

"Eveline! Eveline!" — Madam,
As against the Fine Arts' Dogma
The sad clothes line, or
Your laundered conception
        of the B. V. D.

        Have seen:
That day,
And the Jews eating unleavened bread;

Ramshackle field-weed; —

"— Lie down
I'll marry you!"

        The answer:
Do you think we are sailors?

New are, the trees,
Purple in the violets' swath,
Birds — birds — birds,
Against bark a child's forehead
                tormented red,
(No glasses between eyes and bark)
Face to bark.

        The answer:

Under sky
The winds breathe in the fields.
Standing there chest to chest,

One horse
Walked off,
The trees showing sunlight
Sunlight trees,
Words ranging forms.

6

Environs, the sea of —,
Grace notes, appoggiatura, suspension,
The small note with or without a stroke across the stem;

    Beata Virgo Maria, when sunlight
    Runs over Mrs. Green, may ever
    Her enormous kindness bellow
    To her daughter: "Eveline!"

    Jesus bless, too, that lady's avoirdupois
    Great as of outlasting song,
    Also her tiny daughter hoiden
    Outwriggling the wriggly Wrigley boys.

And those loved seeking their own completion in a
                 voice, their own voice sounding
Melody, sequence
O head, think, how climbing, you would be;
   O heart,
        how
           the
              blood
And the measures (travel outward)
Should travel together;
The mutual slap comes suddenly
After tiredness between people,
Everything lowered to a mutual, common level,
Everyone the same,

Each, at best, obbligato to the other,
Everyone tired of trying to see differences,
Crossed or uncrossed,
Practicing word sleight —
'The sea of necessity, yes,
That stem Atlas carrying his on his shoulder
Should know nothing less than a lightning rod,
Way up, don't ask me where' —

    Saying, It's a hard world anyway,
        Not many of us will get out of it alive.

But who would say —
If this world, the sources,
Fathers, wherever they put their hats,
Spiralled with tessellation as sands of the sea,
The Speech no longer spoken and not even a Wall
                    to worship,
Holy, laundered into a blank and washed over
Tradition's pebbles, the mouth full,
The fugue a music heap,
    only by the name's grace music
(Fate — fate — fate — void   unable to write
                  a melody —
Ludwig and Goethe of one century,
Forms only in snatches,
Words rangeless, melody forced by writing,
Walk, as arms beat in circles, past each other) —

    Would you persist?

Natura Naturans —
Nature as creator,

Natura Naturata —
Nature as created.

>He who creates
>Is a mode of these inertial systems —
>The flower — leaf around leaf wrapped
>>around the center leaf,

>Environs — the sea,
>The ears, doors;
>The words —
>Lost — visible.

>Asked Albert who introduced relativity —
>"And what is the formula for success?"
>"X = work, y = play, Z = keep your mouth
>>shut."
>"What about Johann Sebastian? The same
>>formula."

The song — omits?
No, includes Kay, Anybody.
Ricky's romance
Of twenty-three years, in
Detail, continues

>He — a — pyjamas off —
>Invites ants upon his ankle
>Up-up, ta-ta,
>>minus, but quite there:

>>"I beg your pardon
>>I've a— "h" begins the rhyme here,
>>Shall we now?"

"You misconstrue — uh
Men's rue — eh,
Anyhow!"

The sailors in the carousel
looking for a place to
bury — Ricky;
Seaweed, fellow voters, and
spewn civic sidewalks.

Thus one modernizes
His lute,
Not in one variation after another;
Words form a new city,
Ours is no Mozart's
Magic Flute —
Tho his melody made up for a century
And, we know, from him, a melody resolves
to no dullness —
But when we push up the daisies,
The melody! the rest is accessory:

My one voice. My other: is
An objective — rays of the object brought to a focus,
An objective — nature as creator — desire
for what is objectively perfect
Inextricably the direction of historic and
contemporary particulars.

J. S. B.: a particular,
His Matthew Passion, a particular,
And that other century
Mentioned thru trains' run over trestle

one Easter Sunday:
"Napoleon filled a barrel with rams horns
And sent it to Italy. The Great Boot
Filled a barrel with —
It's hard to say — parts — the men of parts
All but their parts out of the barrel
And sent it to Napoleon —
Stressing, 'This is what *we* did to *your* soldiers!'
And that's history, contention,
A cheeseless mousetrap. Fills up spaced paper."
Another kind of particular.
We are after all realists capable of distinctions.

"Many people are too busy to be unemployed," says
                                        Henry.
(Especially those who have their own factories
                            to take care of.)
"If communism ever gets into a country
And raises Ned with it,
It's because that country needs it.
Only about one family
In ten has a bathtub.
They should be made cheaper,
So that everybody could have them.
If goods don't sell,
It's because they're no good
Or are too high priced."
(Disposed of: the short change of labor.)
As for labor,
"There are more people
Who won't try to do anything",
Says Henry,
"Than there are who don't know what to do,
I am in the business of making automobiles

Because I believe I can do more good that way
Than any other.
Industry itself is a part of culture.
The fact that a man knows a lot
About industry does not prevent
His using good grammar,
Standing straight and appearing well.
We need beauty in everything, and culture
Should be a thing of practice,
Not something apart.
Everything should be a thing of beauty,
Well made and well thought out."

    Spilt from the running-board, Ricky! —
    The buildings rise on the heights,
      Turrets with windows delight
    The ladies garnered in tights
      Of crimson tinseled with
               white.

History: the records of taste and economy of a
                           civilization.
Particular: Every fall season, every spring, he needs
                      a new coat
         He loses his job —
Poetry? it has something to do with his writing of
                         poetry.
"*That*'s poetry," he was told.
"It's fiction, too, isn't it," said Henry,
"I read poetry, and I enjoy it
If it says anything,
But so often it doesn't say anything."

    The common air includes

Events listening to their own tremors,
Beings and no more than breath
                              between them,
Histories, differences, walls,
And the words which bind them no more than
"So that," "and" —
The thought in the melody moves —
A line, flash of photoplay.

        "When you're phosphates,
            They'll look you up and discover —
        J. S. B. was a Latin instructor —
        Some individual you were!",
        Croaked Mr. Anybody.

Tastes: Men of forty kiddin' themselves in blue overalls,
With little blue and red trucks.
Septuagenarian actor's personal locomotive
For retired estate which his boy day dreams realized.
De gustibus bespeaks. . . the sparrow. . . pecking
                              at something unmentionable.

To find a thing, all things.

        On that morning when everything
                will be clear,
        Greeting myself, despite glasses,
        The world's earth a rose,
                rose every particle
        The palm open,
                earth's lily,
        One will see
                gravel in gravel

Stray bits
           of burnt matches
Glass,
           disused rubber,
Scrape heels of shoes,
           and not trip,
Not that one will get, see
           more than particulars,

                    Rest Thee softly, softly rest.

Preparing to receive the captain of industry,
Emptied a full wardrobe and, after he came,
Said — "My dear Magnus, here, entirely to yourself,
's a closet for your suspenders."
The time was —
By Mazola, on Riverside Drive —
The heyday of revivals of western movies,
After the cowboys
Who did their darnest, angels, could do no more.
Seriously,
The young lady, remorseful, having brought scandal
On the family by taking to smoking
Wore the gray stockings again she had always been
                              wearing lately.

And the time was:
The gun shoots — go!
Glory of the Seas by *Free Wash* out of *Tan Seamen*,
vs. *Temper Awake* by *Splashed* out of *Sleep*,
Dogs — I'll grant you dogs —
But a horse,
That's an animal!

The time was:
The same woman, cries the kid,
With the same dog, and
The same man! — gaging her speed.

The time was Arcy Bell:
A nigger
Had a city and a country home
And a rabbit patch on which
 he 'conveniently did shoot them'
In the few hours we were not worked
 in the Post Office together,
He and I and Van — with his projection of
         forehead —
 Dutch, flaxen, slight, plus inherited New England
       seafaring suavity —

 "I dreamt that I tickled my grandfather's aw-awls,
With the oi-oi-ly edge of a feather!

 Arcy agin' the wall!
 Shoot high yaller
 Agin' the wall!"

And it was to the glory of Liza — Arcy's —
And Eliza Jane, his friend's wife
  who was invited only with her husband,
That they paired off always
As individual families,
Having taken over standards that would
Have been impoliteness to Eskimos.

Seriously: As serious as
Four and a half decades kiddin' himself on a

                               miniature golf-course.
I tell you this man had vistas: —
Ties, handkerchiefs to watch,
Mufflers, dress shirts, golf holes,
Chocolate eclaires, automobiles and entrees.

Played polo.
And the — the — the very old stutterers, mumbletypeg
                        in duplex Park Av. apartments,
Mumbling imperceptibly when the jack-knife stuck
                     twenty-five dollar shoe leather.
Their children got jobs because "they didn't believe in
                            Santa Claus,"
Said Henry, "good boys, Uncle Magnus, they come of
                         good families!"
The time was: 'heretical',
The Church identified with aesthetics,
The heretics sought perfection, Blessed Virgin Mary, as tho
    your lips were made out of lipstick,
Their logic the height of your pregnancy.
But, naturally, they were offended for all religions
At the time the Cross heaps were blasted in Moscow.

    "It is more pleasant and more useful,"
    Said Vladimir Ilytch,
    "To live thru the experience
    Of a revolution
    Than to write about it."

The women held the world cornice,
The Red Army was buttressed by women.

The star, Venus, bathed
In the sunsets

        of elegant, imperial islands —
Mr. — 'we own your, this government
benefits by our protection. . . ' —
And in Haiti
Mars
Bloody
Tinkered with the other
Stars.

An accent, not any one nation's
Evidently a matter to attract the next diner.
Not royalty, but faces hollowed as royalty,
A passion growing urban as in Greece, —
A vague dream, — standing each other to drinks,
Aging eyes, impish, overhanging
Carafes on bars
Under leaves serrated in falls,
And at theatricals.
The hands wandering over each other,
A hole and entered.
And above terraces of the city, a hill,
Night, Aldebaran,
Young, no differences in ages, a hole.
'Disturbed?' 'What's in the underbrush?' A white rabbit
Plumped on his belly. Reassured. Thru trees,
White teeth perhaps
Laughed. . .

The time was:
He had worked enough in his pa's wheatfields,
And gone to the State University,
And now participated with the angels in Paris.

The time was:
12 years after Ilytch's statement
When the collectivists
Raised the great metallurgical plants
In Siberia,
For a people's idea,
As well as their practice;
Tariffs;
The U. S. A. embargo
On pulp-wood from Russia,
Tho the U. S. A. needed the pulp-wood.
If there must be nations, why not
Make it clear they're for business?

"We've got to find new uses for wheat," said Henry;
The time was when its shipment would
Have done good to Ivan
                    still waiting for his own tractor —
Kulak unable to see that there was any
Good in anything without any money.

Alfalfa for our horses,
The time for hitch-hikers across country
                    (Summertime).
New York, and then desolation.
The steel works of Gary.
At Lake Michigan in Chicago,
Left a note he was going to Berkeley.

Desolation. Brush. Foothills of the Rockies.
A roof, like a green sea, of a desert shack in Nevada,
120 degrees in the shade —
Far away in the heat the monument of

a city.

Divorced from himself,
Was advised in the night life of Reno:
  "You see this road thru the desert,
  They call it a highway.
  The Lincoln highway.
  It's time this country forked up
  Coin for roads.
  They could if they didn't have prohibition:
  See this spittoon,
  Empty it and there's nothin' in it;
  The Treasury is like a spittoon,
  Except that you've got to fill it with taxes;
  So there's no reason why the poor purchaser
  Shouldn't have his swig as another."

Was advised:
  "It's to laugh
  Bust up automobile parts —
  I had 'em during the war, Henry didn't —
  Just gravy, —
  Did I care?
  I had 'em, kept 'em
  Till they wanted 'em. *You bet* they wanted 'em.
  But in peace times
  You've got to use things,
  Keep 'em in circulation,
  If I ain't got it, the other fellow has. —
  Yes, I'm retired."

Hot n' bothered?

'Ave an ice-cream cone!

Outside the voice of one word:
    "Asunder!"

Then
        "A — sole, a — sole
        A soldier boy was he

        Two — pis   two — pis
        Two pistols on his knee"

Every day's a love day to a sailor,
Who's the boy who would not see the wurrld,
Show me him and I'll show you he's paler
'N yaller b'sides his bunting flag unfurrled

Was told:
        Dem Rooshans ain't rational, why!
        De damn fools would pard'n 'nfanticide
        An' make 't — phwhat nerve! — international —
        Bolshewiki; wher' do they git that stuff —

            "Asunder!"

On that Sunday, in the wind, in the night,
                    in the grasses,
Were prostrated a thousand asses —
Lads' and lasses'.

Achieved:
A country of musty, inherited grants
And aged Indians

Employed to establish
Proof of the grants to the white men:
"Not 150, that can't be your age?"
        Indian's counsel proceeded cautiously,
"No... No...! That wrohng! lheast 200!"

Achieved:
San Francisco's hills and fogs;
In one of its newspapers —
"Some of our best and largest dowagers
                almost do the split";
Sing Fat Co. — merchants.

Across
The Pacific
The roving Red bands of South China,
The poor would give to the poor,
                when incited. Beyond

Parched earth and fog here:
Type of mind faking a thirst for itself —
Land's jest —
Concoctors of 'hard' poetry —
Dramatic stony lips, centaurs, theatrical rock —
Living in a tower beyond rock,
In the best imitation of Sophocles.

While in the sea
The seals pearled for a minute
In the sun as they sank.

Returned,
Three thousand miles over rails,

To adequate distribution of "Camels";
    New York — Staten Island —
Bay water viscous
    where the waves mesh;

To her and
Her mother half-blind;
Stone sculpture, head against white, streaked wall paper,
                          water-marked,
The wood stairway climbing in her child's dream —
The kid at night waking to say
              trai-n, ca-ar,
Or waked to make, "Angel, make."
In the night, Michelangelo, which of your
Sistine angels ever made?
We sang Le Roi Renaud,
Red piano under the stone head,
Or "What can I do to show how much I love" —
Purcell plangent to Dryden's stiff love-making,

"Waken my fair one from thy slumber,"
"The gentle mother that thee bore,"

Or another night,
Mary with us, "Noël est revidici, chantons, Noël, Noël,"
Missing a fireplace.

The frogs all night in Belaire Road,
New York a miniature, steeples not steeples in distance,
At night turret lights not turret lights. By day
Miniature of white spires, roofs,
A bridge. . . cobweb, no, a bridge, if you look hard;

Springtime when the energy under yoke freed,

Wind poking the new green
Is a prelude to the Passion —
"J. S. B., everytime we play that Chorale
The man just stands up."

And to rise in the morning,
Like nothing on earth,
Sounded contacts,
"You must certainly love us to come each Sunday,
What have we
Remembering J. S. B. just stands up?"

The fir trees grew round the nunnery,
The grille gate almost as high as the firs,
Two nuns, by day, passed in black, like
    Hooded cameras, as if photographing
                                    the world.

Cut short the night's work,
Took her to see "Connie's Hot Chocolates",
A new Tanskin Revel
The Hot Chocolate Drops and the Bon Bon Buddies
    dancing
            "off-time"
                    for finale

And she liked it but not enough, and
It really wasn't so good as when I saw
        It the first time,

Nothing's as good as the first time,
But that man Bach just stands up always,

He wrote a Kaffee Cantata
Spelling it "Coffee" as we do (sounded contacts)
A kind of "Hot Chocolates" five years after the Passion,

And not performed till nine years later in Frankfort,
Among strangers — there was always the practical
                    problem of getting an audience:
The Chocolates, for instance, were never too
                        successful in Harlem. —

All about a maiden coffee-bibber —
A hot chocolate we'd say —
Who had to three times daily
Coffee drink, is the German,

            Beginning
Schweigt still — plaudert nicht —
Quiet — cut the gab —
No "please" in the German —
That to his audience.

Forgetting
        I said:
                Can
                The design
                Of the fugue
                Be transferred
                To poetry?

        At eventide

            Venus come up

How shall I —
Her soles new as the sunned black of her grave's turf,

With all this material
                    To what distinction —

7

Horses: who will do it? out of manes? Words
Will do it, out of manes, out of airs, but
They have no manes, so there are no airs, birds
Of words, from me to them no singing gut.
For they have no eyes, for their legs are wood,
For their stomachs are logs with print on them;
Blood red, red lamps hang from necks or where could
Be necks, two legs stand A, four together M.
"Street Closed" is what print says on their stomachs;
That cuts out everybody but the diggers;
You're cut out, and she's cut out, and the jiggers
Are cut out. No! we can't have such nor bucks
   As won't, tho they're not here, pass thru a hoop
   Strayed on a manhole — me? Am on a stoop.

Am on a stoop to sit here tho no one
Asked me, nor asked you because you're not here,
A sign creaks — LAUNDRY TO-LET
                  (creaks — wind —) — SUN —
(Nights?) the sun's, bro', what month's rent in arrear?
Aighuh — and no manes and horses' trot? butt, butt
Of earth, birds spreading harps, two manes a pair
Of birds, each bird a word, a streaming gut,
Trot, trot — ? No horse is here, no horse is there?
Says you! Then I—fellow me, airs! we'll make
Wood horse, and recognize it with our words —
Not it — nine less two! — as many as take
To make a dead man purple in the face,

Full dress to rise and circle thru a pace
Trained horses — in latticed orchards, (switch!) birds.

Just what I said — Birds! — *See Him! Whom?*
                                    The Son
Of Man, grave-turf on taxi, taxi gone,
Who blabbed of orchards, strides one leg here, one
Leg there — wooden horses? give them manes! —
                                    (was on
A stoop, *He found them sleeping*, don't you see?)
See him! How? Against wood his body close,
Speaks: My face at where its forehead might be,
The plank's end 's a forehead waving a rose —

Birds — birds — nozzle of horse, washed plank in air...
For they had no manes we would give them manes,
For their wood was dead the wood would move — bare
But for the print on it — for diggers gone, trains'
    Run, light lights in air where the dead reposed —
    As many as take liveforever, "Street Closed".

"Closed"? then fellow me airs, We'll open ruts
For the wood-grain skin laundered to pass thru,
Switch is a whip which never has been, cuts
Winds for words — Turf streams words, airs untraced
                                    — New
The night, and orchards were here? Horses passed? —
    There were no diggers, bro', no horses there,
    But the graves were turfed and the horses grassed —
Two voices: — Airs? No birds. Taxi? No air —

Says one! Then I — Are logs?! Two legs stand "A" —
Pace them! in revolution are the same!

Switch! See! we can have such and bucks tho they
Are not here, nor were there, pass thru a hoop
(Tho their legs are wood and their necks 've no name)
Strayed on a manhole — See! Am on a stoop!

See! For me these jiggers, these dancing bucks:
Bum pump a-dumb, the pump is neither bum
Nor dumb, dumb pump uh! hum, bum pump o! shucks!
(Whose clavicembalo? bum? bum? te-hum...)
Not in the say but in the sound's — hey-hey —
The way to-day, Die, die, die, die, tap, slow,
Die, wake up, up! up! *O Saviour*, to-day!
Choose Jews' shoes or whose: anyway Choose! Go!

But they had no eyes, and their legs were wood!
But their stomachs were logs with print on them!
Blood red, red lamps hung from necks or where could
Be necks, two legs stood A, four together M —
  They had no manes so there were no airs, but —
  Butt... butt... from me to pit no singing gut!

Says you! Then I, Singing, It is not the sea
But what floats over: hang from necks or where could
Be necks, blood red, red lamps (Night), Launder me,
Mary! Sea of horses that once were wood,
Green and, and leaf on leaf, and dancing bucks,
Who take liveforever! Taken a pump
And shaped a flower. "Street Closed" on their stomachs.
But the street has moved; at each block a stump
That blossoms red, And I sat there, no one
Asked me, nor asked you. Whom? You were not there.
A sign creaked — LAUNDRY TO-LET — (creaked —
                    wind --) — SUN --

(Nights?) the sun's, bro', no months' rent in arrear —
   Bum pump a-dum, no one's cut out, pump a-
   Ricky, bro', Shimaunu-Sān, yours is the

Clavicembalo — Nine less two, Seven
Were the diggers, seven sang, danced, the paces
Seven, Seven Saviours went to heaven —
Their tongues, hands, feet, eyes, ears and hearts,
                                        each face as
Of a Sea looking Outward (Rose the Glass
Broken), Each a reflection of the other.
Just for the fun of it. And 't came to pass

       (*Open, O fierce flaming pit!*)

                              three said: "Bother,

Brother, we want a meal, different techniques."
Two ways, my two voices... Offal and what
The imagination... And the seven came
To horses seven (of wood — who will? — kissed
                                        their stomachs)
Bent knees as these rose around them — trot — trot —
Spoke: words, words, we are words, horses, manes,
                                        words.

8

And of labor:
Light lights in air,
    on streets, on earth, in earth —
Obvious as that horses eat oats —
    Labor as creator,
      Labor as creature,
To right praise.

   THREE HOURS
    AGONY
   IN THIS CHURCH
   GOOD FRIDAY

To provide the two Choirs the work demanded
He employed his *chorus primus* and *chorus*
      secundus
Choruses comparatively simple,
Within the competence of singers
Not called on to sing figural music,
The Thomaskirche could provide the two organs
    the score prescribes,
(The larger, in the west gallery, a two-manual
    instrument)
Two orchestras composed of the town's musicians,
Players in the Thomasschule, University *studiosi*,
And members of Bach's Collegium Musicum

"Pray we our Lord"

High officials and well-born ladies,
With devotion,
    joining to sing the first Choral from their
                              books:
But as the theatrical music proceeded —
    "What does it all mean?"
One old lady, a widow: 'God help us!
'Tis surely a comic-Opera!'

    'Natural that Bach should enjoy himself,
    Had of course to play his music in church'

And out of respect for what he said about Bach,
  and the need for amusement in church,
One would salute with two fingers,
Out of respect (tho one has known respect
                        before)
    two fingers:
             which
Touch, sign from, the forehead,
The personal clarity, after the voice known
                  has spoken.
  "How journeyed?"
Journeyed.
With impulse to master
music and related matters.
Others agonizing, inside all their lives but
                  never really,
Kept quick notations for cages of song,
Peered thru the cages to see the yellow,
               by night light,
To hear sounds sweeter than by day,

By day already exceeded by the instant.

Not Joh. Seb. Bach, Director Musices:
A short and much-needed statement of the
requirements of church
music. With some general reflections
on its decline:
To perform concerted music as it should be
rendered,
both singers and instrumentalists are required.
. . no one cares to work for nothing.
. . in the *chorus secundus* I am obliged to use
scholars otherwise available
. . *beneficia*, themselves inconsiderable, formerly
available for the *chorus musicus* have
been withdrawn.
It is astonishing that . . musicians should
be expected
to play *ex tempore* any music put before
them,
. . the necessity to earn their . . bread
allowing them little leisure to perfect their
technique,
. . observe how the royal musicians . . are paid.

Friends too tired to see differences,
This, Marx dissociated:
"*Equal* right . . presupposes inequality,
Different people are *not* equal one to another."
But to make the exploitation by one man of many
impossible!
When the opposition between brain and manual work
will have disappeared,

When labor will have ceased to be a mere means of
                                    supporting life,

    Whether it was 'impossible for matter to think?'
            Duns Scotus posed.
    Unbodily substance is an absurdity
            like unbodily body. It is impossible
    to separate thought and matter that thinks.

"Described", in *Das Kapital*, "large-scale industry
Not only as the mother of antagonism, but as the
                                    producer
Of the material and spiritual conditions for resolving
                            that antagonism. .
It is true the solution cannot proceed along pleasant
                                    lines."

    Infinite is a meaningless word: except — it states
    The mind is capable of performing
            an endless process of addition.

            Who by construction have
            A bird settling like a leaf
            Will bury Lord Jesu

            For labor who will sing
            When spring, the May,
            Is strength enough?

            The mirth of all this land
            Browne, Morel and More
            (Who speed the plow in May!)

Rewarded with a sheaf or more
Of an
         evening —

The poor

Betrayed and sold.

No thought exists
Completely abstracted from action,
Without the solids of bodies
There is no geometry,
Who acknowledge space — moving
Know as many dimensions
                    as they have muscles

Who have signed to the probability
Of a series of 8 red planes,
Not 7 followed by a black,
         Greet the arrivals in their veins,
Know whatever news the future brings to the world
Should have one constant: Name? — perhaps Energy.
                    Sure, if the flight
Becomes more and more penetrating
The simple will be discovered beneath the complex
Then the complex under the simple
Then again the simple under the complex
And, and, the chain without sight of the last term,
                              etc., Etc.,

The facts are not strange to each other.
When they drive, your choice
Cannot but be guided by simplicity.

Not enough to reject the falsely related,
The mirrors of the facts must not be dis-
                                        simulated:

In the advertisement
One handle of a toothbrush lasts a lifetime,
But brush your teeth of their tartar and
Reenamel the handle.

Two legs stand —
                    Pace them

Railways and highways have tied
Blood of farmland and town
    And the chains
    Speed wheat to machine
This is May
The poor's armies veining the earth!

Hirers once fed by the harried
Cannot feed them their hire
    Nor can chains
    Hold the hungry in
This is May
The poor are veining the earth!

Light lights in air blossoms red
Like nothing on earth
    Now the chains
    Drag graves to lie in
This is May
The poor's armies veining the earth!

March
From hirer unchained
   Till your gain
   Be the
World's

To this end, Communists assembled in London
Sketched the Manifesto of the party itself.
Hidden, open fight — to date that is history:
Exploiting and exploited. When in the ice-age
A pipe made of a lion's tooth played D and G,
Or when glass harmonica or dining table
Tuned their glass (plunged tones) there was history
                                        (movement
In excavations) an economy that is,
Which was the material clef of the music.

A column against which the whole ensemble leans
Should the struck bars of oblong glass be stopped —
                                        a void
To be felt (Why does Monsieur P. talk about God) —
The music brings up a vacuum thru which light
Travels — (as a hesitant voice comes up to fact)
Light-wave and quantum, we have good proof both exist:
Our present effort is to see how this is: to
Perfect the composition of a two-point view,
The economists have a similar problem.

Light above shifting heads, inertia of light.
Thought is weightless but is stopped by a bullet, what?
Call its quick, least particle a system of waves,

Build it. Designate by ψ that "something", changes
In which trident stay responsible for the waves,
Thought has assumed what thought is compelled to
                                             assume!
Bearings, a choice of facts, impetus imparted
By conflict; history does not begin again
When a thought trains on the fact that begins again.

Lollai, lollai, litil child, Whi wepistou so?
For the estates Mentula had, that you will have?
Lollai, lollai, litil child, Child, lolai, lullow!
Now drinkes he up seas, and he eates up flocks, He's but
A coof for a' that: he'll break his whip that guiltlesse
Smals must die — I spec it will be all 'fiscated.
De massa run, ha! ha! De darkey stay, ho! ho!
So distribution should undo excess — (chaseth),
Shall brothers be, be a' that, Child, lolai, lullow.

When the sheriffe see gentle Robin wold shoote, held
Up both his hands. As defeats gaged economies,
Lags when gallows looped distance, the Manifesto:
That quantum of the means of subsistence which leaves
No surplus to command the labor of others,
The Communists see no need to abolish that,
Growth of industry is destroying it daily;
You must allow by "individual" is meant
Middle-class owner, not nine-tenths of the people.

I saw my lady weep, the glass harmonica
Stilled — society splitting into two camps, two
Classes, light but the common's sun, with Elberfeld's
Rich gone Communist (Engels), Bach's double chorus
Not paid a herring, eight themes spacing eight voices,
Thought as axes of bodies, labor sold piecemeal,

Masses of laborers, crowded, factories, slaves
Of class, Marx Englished, Woodhull and Claflin's Weekly,
Phase, the pit, Marx waiting, time to go, said Adams.

Thought eighty years — a void in which nothing was
                                        dead —
And if he could come back — Henry Adams — to see
The mistakes plain in light of the new — one had seen:
The state can either take or borrow; seventy
Million tons of coal fall past the past down the chutes
Leashed to capital; ash-heaps; Viollet-le-Duc's
Guess—edifices of steel, stone sheathes preserving
Them — built as guessed. Silver slipped across the
                                        chasm. Light?
What is light? physicists failed. Gold? politics' light.

All one's best citizens the banks, — the first May Day
Who had whistled? The scale fell as the pail emptied.
Can the middle-classes pay the scale, play the scale?
What do *you* think — with the state's gold safe in
                                        a vault
To be flooded in case of war? I asked the boss
Why my crops were his. He said the coal bill; you took
Off the Fourth of July. Subdivided shops, fire
Hazards. The evicted dawdle, the shots hit home.
My kid's bare as a plucked bird's hole in whistling time.

Proletarians massed on each nation's curtain
Of fire, fighting to stop the haggling of nations,
The void fills, the music of old glass is playing new
Announcements of economies, As one object
Speeding in the light in a calculus of speed,
Revolution is the pod systems rattle from,
Yet no frame breaks being elastic, the column

Of the wake continues into the wave, Disdain
To shunt aims, To each his needs, the Manifesto.

Heat, not substance.   Simmer, not wraith.
Battle drains off like work; unavailable energy increases.
He is passive, sure to be broken down.
Shorter along the line of motion, than across
The line of motion, contraction depending on speed —
The hummingbird inmate of thought
An incident here: angle of a light's reflection
Altered by the motion of a mirror.

The hummingbird: rubythroat.
170 meters of the wall collapsed.

The sun — over all things.
He hairs his views.

Who will say the last, the man's dying, lines are vague?
Look up at the mist on trees.
Arrangements: the trickles
Swung machine-guns in deadly arcs

To-day
The motor; the transmission mechanism; the working
machine.

Fly back mowed down, into the hills, over the horses,
You speeds, terrestrial bodies, that have outrun our
automobiles.
Voice a voice blown: print

Must not overlap, but the notes of the voices would.

The cultured growth is scrapped.

> Au nom
> de la République
> vous êtes décorés
> de la croix de l'Ordre
> des Feuilles Mortes.

"Theory is grey, my friend.   But green — !"
"Petrov, the shot was an accident?"
"Accident?!   I stepped forward, loaded, took aim."

Nor advocate 'waiting' until the troops 'come over'.

"An eight hour day *and* arms!"

The siege of the Aquarium,
an open-air restaurant.
The crowd, attacked by the dragoons,
Unorganized, absolutely spontaneously, but hesitatingly
Set up — .
Ten-, three-, or even two-men detachments.

The whole population is in the streets
Network of barricades.

— that rebellion is an art.
Take it from me, what we need
Is fitness, not suffusion.
To drink the stinking source of some French 'positivists'
Is too much.

You're right there on the spot ..
I do not know the nature of A. M. ch's writing at
                                              present,

Nor his working capacity ..
· If you think we shall not harm his work
By harnessing him .. it would be criminal
If such trifles as journalism should disrupt
                              serious work ..

The every-day exchange relation need not. be directly
Identical with the magnitudes of value.

The exchequer of the poor.
Of all the arts the wind can blow
The most important, in my opinion, is the cinema.

Sorry we have to have strikes, but
The whole theory of the use of gas is
It makes it unnecessary to use bullets.
I have been gassed myself at least 1,000 times
The company is constantly
              experimenting on its own people.

What is said to be the first motion picture in America,
Made in 1870, it was called "Diaphanous",
And shown in the opera houses.
One reel depicted the Minnesota Massacre,
The other a "news reel" of the time
Will be shown as when it duly
Sobered and horrified the gentlemen
And made small children gasp
And hide their faces in their mothers' shawls
And the women softly weep.

Flanagan and Phepoe
Lottery & Insurance Office
Next door but one to Fly Market

No. 151 Water St., New York,
One hundred sometime years ago:
A superb Double Cased Gold Watch
                        Chances sixpence
Unequalled Policies by which the Holder
   has 4 chances of obtaining 50,000 dollars
& 100 dollars, if last drawn.
These unparalleled advantages to be obtained
For the truly trifling risque of one shilling:
Now is your time,
Choose a firm Cloud before it falls, and in it
Catch e'er she die, the Cynthia of the Minute

Fresh as a daisy and as dirty.

The 300 years banishment of Roger Williams
from Massachusetts ended officially to-day.
Governor C with a stroke of his pen
Rescinded the decree of the Bay Colony's Court
Which in (let it pass) gave the outspoken
Radical of his day 6 months to leave.
On Monday the governor will present to Rhode Island
In person a copy and so forth of the bill he
                        signed to-day.

Whoobsx struck me much like a steam-engine
In trousers white above pylons.

So dry the sloughs and water holes when the rain came

It did little more than to moisten their bottoms.
A motorist occasionally stops along the road
To scrape the battered bodies of grasshoppers
                    from his windshield and radiator,
The pest creeping and flying. Only the Russian thistle
Is green for the eye in this state, but to be of use
It must be cut while green.   As yet it is too short
                                    for cutting.
Farmers and ranchers crowd the offices of
                    county agents and welfare boards.
A tan moss so close to the ground, hungry cattle cannot
                                    reach it.

Process: notion about which the researches cluster.
The knowledge sought and the manner of seeking it
Are a product of the cultural growth.
All the generalities on motion belong here.
Ions, together with what is known of the obscure
                    and late-found — .
In so far as the science is of modern complexion,
In so far as it is not of the nature of taxonomy simply,
The inquiry converges upon a matter of process,
And it comes to rest,
Provisionally, when it has disposed of the process.
Whereas it is claimed that scientific inquiry
Neither does nor can legitimately, nor, indeed, currently
Make use of a postulate more metaphysical
Than the concept of an idle concomitance of variation,
                                    such
As is adequately expressed in terms of mathematical
                                    function.

Consistently adhered to, the principle of "function"
Or concomitant variation

Precludes recourse to experiment, hypothesis or
                                    inquiry — indeed
It precludes "recourse" to anything whatever. Its
                                    notation (however)
Does not comprise anything so anthropomorphic.

I am now working like a horse (Marx)
As I must use the time in which it is possible
                                    to work
And the carbuncles are still here
Tho now they disturb me only locally
And not in the brain pan.
One cannot always be writing (*Das Kapital*)
I am doing some differential calculus —
the derivative of x with respect to y —
I have no patience to read anything else
Other reading always drives me back to my writing.
Then there is still the fourth book, the historical-literary,
                                    to write —
The easiest for me as the problems have been solved
                                  in the first three
And this is repetition.

. . damnable iteration . . art able to corrupt a saint.

— repetition. I cannot bring myself to send anything
Till I have the whole before me.
As to this "damned" book . .

This evening a special session of the International.
A good fellow, an old Owenist, Weston (carpenter)
Continually defending two propositions in *The Beehive*:
— That a general rise in the rate of wages
would be of no use to workers
— That therefore, etc., the trade unions

are *harmful*. —
If these two propositions, in which *he*
Alone in our society believes, were accepted,
We would become a joke to the trade unions

(in England)
And because of the strikes now on the Continent.
I should have written out my reply
But thought it more urgent to work at my book,
So shall have to improvise.

The Jacob Grimm method more suited to works

not constructed.

Or that science is an art.
Each art a science

"does not need any philosophy

towering above the other sciences."

Technology throws light upon mental conceptions.
"intervals of gradualness."
Quantity into quality.
Or sweetness: where there is more light than logic.
A full number of things in a very few words.

To be sure .. so thoroughly aware of merits .. as I trust
We are and always shall be ..

"To sponge in a brook
before sunrise with the thermometer at thirty
and a bracing breeze blowing,
tries the epidermis"

Bomb-Face the racketeer,

With a bodyguard's pistols watching each ear
Wanting to rub everything out
Beer-runner Bum-Face and legitimate business
Directed his boys as he entered the Ritziest Joint —
If I Should Tell My Love My Pen Would Burn:
Rub out that music.
He made no distinctions.

First time witt repetition!
Two time witt repetition!
Three time witthout repetition!
Wit-hout!   Wit-hout!   Wit-hout!

And he said: *Der Lenin hat anders getan.*
Went to the apothecary and he said:
You like your business, yet it keeps you in
Twenty-four of twenty-four hours a day.
How would you like it. if for the first time in
                                    twenty-four years
You take a well-earned vacation
                              for six months,
While the shop continues as yours
Managed by four qualified youngsters
Each working six-hour daily shifts
During that time?
You say qualified, asked the apothecary?   Alright.
And he went and took his vacation
Under the NEP
And mind you there he was after only six weeks vacation
Satisfied with his qualified helpers
And content to work the six-hour shift himself,
While his son grew up under the Second
                              Five Year Plan.
And one day when the youngster was already

an engineer

He said: paPA, do you really think this

pharmacy is ours?

You know, it's really the state's.

And both realized and had a good time

over their combined situation.

He (Lenin) came to this earth, to drive

out Kuchak, Tajiks!

Kuchak (Adam).

He slays the dragon, with golden arms

Born of the moon and the stars,

When the world was made he helped, too

Comrades of Uzbekistan.

The strength of one man can be reckoned

1/20 of a horsepower —

Think then, 10 turbines are 900,000 horsepower.

The gas flame of the autogenic welder

burns thru steel

And is not put out by water.

And the veins of the earth, and the veins

of a leaf,

And the ribs of the human body are like

each other —

Notice the fluoroscope!

If you know all the qualities of a thing

You know the thing itself;

Nothing remains but the fact

The said thing exists without us;

And when your senses have taught

you that fact,
You have grasped the last remnant
of the thing in itself.

"What I did" said Marx, "was to prove"
One) that the existence and war of the classes
Springs from the means of production
Further) that class war brings on of itself
The dictatorship of the proletariat
Last) (and without repetition)
This dictatorship dies, is the end
of the classes.

But the labor process —
Consider the labor process apart
From its particular form under particular
social conditions.
What distinguishes any worker from the best
of the bees
Is that the worker builds a cell in his head
before he constructs it in wax.
The labor process ends in the creation of a thing,
Which when the process began
Already lived as the worker's image.
And he realizes his own purpose
To which he gives up his will.
Nor does he give it up to the crick of
a second
But the less attractive he finds the work in itself,
The less it frees him body and mind —
The more is his care glued to the grind.

Spins and the product is his web
And he can't catch fish in waters where

there are none.
Not used .. is cotton wasted.
Must seize on these things
Must rouse them from their "death-like" sleep.
Bathed in the fire of labor
Brought into contact with living labor
Things animated, consumed, but consumed
for a purpose
In which living labor is itself consumed.

But the rage of an age —
Whether a Cincinnatus conducts
the labor process by tilling his little farm,
Or whether Tom Dick
Wears his vest in summer
And sells refrigerators to the Eskimos —
In bad form the surfaces and planes
all come to an end.

By the green waters oil
The air circles the wild flower; the men
Skirt along the skyscraper street and carry weights
Heavier than themselves;
By the rotted piers where sunk slime feeds
the lily-pads,
Not earth's end.
The machines shattering invisibles
And which wrecked the still life
Precede the singling out; the setting up of things
Upholds the wrist's force; and
The blood in the ear
Direction of the vertical

           rigidly bound to the head, the
           accelerated motion
           of rotation of the head
Under the head's hair.
SOCONY will not always sign off on this air.

Treeless .. sight, sight .. labor's imaginable
                                    house ..
Not the dark, no .. the sun picks this
                              ticking object ..
He is an old man whose lips whisper
                    an infantile verse:
I-was-early-taught-to-work-as-well-as-play-
My-life-has-been-one-long-happy-holiday-
Full-of-work-full-of-play-
I-dropped-the-worry-by-the-way-
And G-g-g-God-was-good-to-me-every-day.

The history of a chair .. old, blue eyes ..
Sure .. I am Mickey Mouse .. why do
   you have to ask .. ?
Proof that .. a .. ancestor of Mickey Mouse ..
Egypt's blue strokes in the papyrus.
J. D. One, and sits in his chair ..
Old Egypt's children .. watching their parents eating ..
North (temperate) the freight goes out by still hangars.
He owns .. even-before-you-begin-
To-prepare-to-start-to-commence-to-
Consider-it-a-vast share in
All-the gas stations of Europe.

What we eat actually is radiation

Of various wave-lengths:
The rays of lightning of the shortest wave-length
Synthesize the nitrogen fraction of food;
The sun's rays of the longer wave-lengths,
The carbon fractions;

Heat and calories,
Lime, phosphorus and vitamin "A".
When industry brought with it
The factories in the valleys
And it-began-to-be-considered-desirable
That the cheese show eyes in the cut
And after, for that "little bite" to complete the
                              evening's enjoyment
The tinfoil wrapper absolutely odorless even in
                              summer,
The moist cold air currents persisted in the caves.
30 to 40 days during which each cheese was scraped,
Then pierced with a multitude of fine steel needles
For the air to reach the bread crumb layers,
So the green mold grew.

Peter's garden, Padre,
The garden above Peter's face,
Green, yellow,
The eyes rolled
The keys
To the heavens.

The Museum (New York) owns little of Bosch, but for
The Virgin's peacock hair.
The pearl sexes, the prepuce-leaves,
Of the old and original establishments of
                              Europe —
They remain in the galleries of Brussels.

Not in the importing offices of — .
America's homes for years missed,
Still miss, that rich accustomed flavor
So unique and prized.

In our times when the producers
Have nothing to consume,
Because there are no consumers,
The blood-purifying properties of this cheese
(Dating back to the 10th century
and made in conical moulds in the Canton
                              of Glarus)
Is a boon to the gourmets of the world.
And this the surface of which
Is colored with litmus in alkaline water
And the other bearing the imprint of a horse's head,
The trade-mark of the original manufacturer.

Bottle-shaped, too, the loaves tied in pairs
With strings and suspended from the ceiling —
To be found in the down town grocery store —
And this cheese frequently turned
                        to retain its shape.

Like and unlike whom —
Who but my Lady Greensleeves
Who lived so long
And loved so long, so long ago,
Whose sleep has no divisions
Who played her role,
Constant,
Re-furbelowing La Fontaine's *Fables*.
In the need (he said for Blue Ontario's Shore)
He or she is greatest

Who contributes the greatest practical example.

What for, when the producers have nothing to consume?
But rather than stand by epileptic, humble, if not
                                                    ashamed,
Forgetting how Hosea approached a Jerusalem of whores!
Yes, if people *could* only read
Not the same as *would* only read
When the crazed burn books — how, read?
"What can you do about it?"

Deprive them of their deeds.

This linen table napkin — needlework in blue
Made in America —
Sharecropper's or marble striker's grandmother's
                                            table napkin
Is as good to us as Breughel's *Harvesters.*
Its landscape depicts a bull,
Quaint, a linen bull.
No, it does not give milk.

So the paintings hang by braided cords in the museum
So much cheese .. so much work ..
Quiet because of the form.   (Or unquiet.)
Breughel copied by Cranach .. to Quentin Matsys.
Hieronymus Bosch—a round of horses,
"Garden of Terrestrial Lust":
The first brains of this party.
Pitting
Greater passion against relentless fury
We had to treat some of our comrades roughly,

I too (Stalin), painters, had a part in this.
So that the brush will not be a mere
                              means of feeding brains.

Technic *was* everything.
Personnel *is* everything.
Having learned technic is everything,
And not to be mired in the next step.

"Adoration of Kings":
The crown on the ground,
The tray with jewelled tumbler offered by hands.
The dog at mother's feet.   The child.
The dog's painted with the same care as the worshippers.
Over: the angels spread a protecting blanket.
To broken masonry from the height of a road in
                the far mountains
Two beggars have come, and warm
Their hands thru a hole serving for window
Over a fire's blue and red on the inside.
Beggars or herdsmen: found their way
Into the picture signed Bosch.   Made *them*
His subject, and not his struggle between "know,
Visitors, by these novel presents and ideal reality"
                              . . Instead
Integration: painted a Simpleton to sweeten him.
Painted also the Adoration — Bluesleeves
Is my heart of gold.
Hangs: — while 40 streets down hung Vincent's
Miners, the very painting of your fear,
Those that we bury back,
In shags, Eight kings followed by Banquo's ghost —
A cold morning in the Borinage;
Like the miners in Pecs, 1000 feet down in the pits,

Shouting up their demands,
58¢ a day or we cut off the air pumps
                    AND ChOkE!
The homicide rate's highest in Nevada,
16.5 per 100,000. But Pecs' average was higher.
1,156 men, all for one, struck for death.

Each night I kiss these buds, my sweet's, birds,
And break an electric bulb with a pick-ax.

Budapest was darkened!

Now *he*'s strung up
He should have stood in bed.

The temperature between a cigarette
And a style in bed
Makes history.
Nineteen kilometers in the stratosphere,
Further than Podolsk is from Moscow,
Three kilometers above the record
                    they made in Europe.
And the little boy said:
Three kilometers above Europe —
We have caught up with
Them, passed them this time.

Due at unwalled porticos, weighing what shores
Who will build with childlike delight?
That child's words will be echoed by millions.
Stratostat a tiny silver globule
Shone, and the dense mass of people,
The little son perched on a shoulder, legs white
Tender like a frog's legs.

Waves of caps to 22 automobiles and trucks
Home from the Central Asian Desert.
Like the balloon, *Stratostat*, the automobiles:
Each part of Soviet make.

"It is ours." Our balloon. Our automobiles. Our trucks.
From the dust of eighty-six days, 5,721 miles.
Blazoned with red flags. Party-colored flowers.

          Dear friend, when
          I die, but
          I'm not dead.

Song?
After bread.

In the stratosphere the color of the sky
Would be a deep soft violet he said.
And he was right. With a chromatic scale of colors
                    we saw the sky,
We did not, as we had expected, see
The curvature of the earth.
Our instruments may yet record it,
The naked eye could not.

Possibly we'll bear witness
To long distance flights at terrific speeds
In altitudes where resistance of air-pressure's
Reduced to a minimum:
But come back to the Soviet after ten years
To see what we shall have done.

If they who have spoken and speak of "armed peace"
Can come back.

If the "foe of mankind," England,
Can come back.
If the diplomats who lie for "the fatherland,"
Pacifists in concentration camps, can come back.
If the wealth of nations' pockets
Can come back.

If the historian cares for his truths,
He is certain to falsify his facts.
Rapprochement with an aggressor is
Like rapprochement of the lobster
With the shark, the lobster hopes
The shark will not eat it all,
Only one claw.
More difficult than to a lobster is the casting of
its shell
Is the *vis inertia* of class history.

Till when labor will have ceased
To be a mere means of supporting life.

People: the most valuable of all capital.

1648. New York in Dutch times
Wages of Indians ordered to be paid
Without disputing their accounts.

1655. All Jews are ordered to depart
From this place.

Circa 100 years later
Rules of this Tavern:
4 pence a night for bed
6 pence for supper

No more than 5 to sleep in one bed
No boots to be worn in the bed
Organ grinders to sleep in the wash house
No dogs allowed upstairs
No beer allowed in the kitchen
No razor grinders or tinkers taken in.

Put away your green paper accordion:
The minuet 's all night from our windows.
The valley bridged by this viaduct is
The Hollow Way of General Washington's time —
Who chopped his father's face
    Into the cherry tree.

Workingmen in Boston and New York —
Their Committee of Mechanics —
Refused to carry on work of erecting fortifications
To close ports to rebels.

"Don't Tread on Me!"
Tom Jefferson defender of the Shaysites.

Washington to the Jewish congregation at Newport:
May the children .. of Abraham
Who dwell in this land continue to merit
And enjoy the good-will of the other inhabitants ..
Every one shall sit under his own
                vine and fig tree ..
Shall be none to make him afraid.

Constructive centralization .. not indeed precisely
At the point at which Washington left it.
"Light-houses of the skies," John Quincy Adams ..

something
Of awful enjoyment .. observing the rising and
setting of the sun .. that
Perpetual revolution of the Great and Little Bear
round the pole;
Orion from .. horizontal .. to .. perpendicular ..
Of sorrow in reflecting how little we can ever know
of it .. of
Almost desponding hope that we may know more
of it ..

As cold as Nova Zembla.
In the morning awakened by the hail — the
Train frozen to the rails
Could not be broken free for an hour.
I felt as if I were incrusted in a bed of snow.

Four of us slept, feet to feet
Next to a stable bulging with horses,
The boat staggered, a stumbling nag.

The Schleswig-Holsteiners, the Anglo-Saxons that is,
Their descendants in England and America
Are not to be converted by lecturing ..
Have got to experience it
on their bodies.
Yet, like everything in America,
Once the first step has been taken,
Some requisite fire under the Schleswig-Holstein
Anglo-Saxons,
Who are usually so slow; and then too
The foreign elements in the nation
Will assert themselves by greater mobility.

Democracy would not permit John Quincy Adams
The ablest staff of officials, to be chosen by him,
To administer the public trust.
It is the system of averages or of levelling downward.
The wage fixed according to the capacity of the
                                         feeblest workman ..
As the pace of the regiment is fixed by the walk
                                 of the slowest horse.

Destroying everything of which I had planted the
                                     germ ..
A forest of live-oak near Pensacola, ..
Because? the natural history of the live-oak
Had many singularities and had not been observed; ..

1828.   American Workingmen's Party
Fighting bank notes and their monopoly.

Animated things and they move in the dark.
                              In the light.
Trees, flatness, houses limited to place,
The flowers' names, the imported trees,
Birds in vines, cut-up lots, kids in blue, their
Dungarees tagging train-dust.

               QUIET
          is requested for
          the benefit of
        those who have re-
               tired.

Who says it, what said, to whom?

Cardanus, for example, wrote about the construction
of clocks:
It would be possible to show from the development
of the clock
How entirely different the relation between theoretical
learning
And practice was in the handicraft,
From what it is in large-scale industry.

The clock and the corn-mill
(The water-mill, that is,)
The clock, the idea of applying automatic device
(Moved by springs) to production.
The mill the essential organism of a machine:
The mechanical driving power; the transmitting
mechanism; the working machine,
Which deals with the material.   Each
With an existence independent of the others.
The mathematicians, so far as they occupied themselves
With practical mechanics and its theoretical side,
Started from the simple corn-grinding water-mill.
The actual work .. beating, crushing, grinding,
pulverisation ..
Was performed from the first *without* human labor
Even tho the moving· force was human or animal.
This kind of machinery is therefore very ancient,
At least in its origins, and
Actual mechanical propulsion was
formerly applied to it.
The German asses .. great at these small things ..
Calling the use of animal power machinery ..
Decided a plough is a machine ..
While the spinning-jenny, in so far as it is

worked by hand, is not.

Jacques de Vaucanson influenced the
        imagination of the English inventors
(With an automatic flute player, with a
Hissing snake which threw itself
On the breast of Cleopatra.
Made Royal Inspector of Silk Manufactures
                by Cardinal Fleury
Vaucanson perfected many machines for
                his industry.) —
1863. Marx to Engels.

The way the North is conducting war . .
Might have been expected
Where fraud . . king so long . .
The South . . where productive work falls
                on the niggers
Is better adapted to it.
All the same I would bet my head . .
These fellows will get the worst of it
In spite of 'Stonewall' Jackson.
All Lincoln's Acts . .
                conditions
One lawyer puts to another.
Does not alter their historic content.
I am even amused when I compare them with the
                drapery
In which a Frenchman envelops even the most
                unimportant point.

Parisian gentlemen . .
Babble science and know nothing,

Scorn all *revolutionary* action
Which can be carried by *political means*
as the *legal* limitation of the working day
1866. Still Marx. I was very pleased
With the American Workers' Congress at Baltimore . .
Curiously enough most of the demands
                    which I drew up for Geneva
Were also put forward there (in Baltimore.)

1869. A Chapter of Erie. C. F. Adams (Jr.).
Ten o'clock the astonished police . . panic-stricken
                                    railway directors . .
In their hands . . files of papers . . and their pockets
Crammed . . assets and securities . . One,
Captain, in a hackney-coach . . with him . . six
                    millions in greenbacks.
Under cover of night . . to the Jersey ferry.
Some . . not daring publicity . . in open boats
Concealed by darkness and a March fog . .
A majority of the Executive Committee
Collected at the Erie Station in Jersey City,
(Ribbed Gothic and grilled iron)
Proceeded to the transaction of business.
Doll said: "A captain!
God's light . . the word as odious as the word
                                    'occupy' . .
Excellent . . before it was ill sorted."
The old maxim of the common law,
That corporations have no souls.
Corporate life and corporate power,
As applied to industrial development,
. . yet in its infancy.
It tends always to development, —

Always to consolidation . .
Even threatens the central government.
It is a new power, for which our language
Contains no name.
(a river that would seem to hang from a tree
Flood valleys, the sky between hung trees and
                            caved arches,
Thru crashed firs red radish half-plugged).
The people . . seek protection against it . .
Look for such protection, significantly enough,
Not to their . . legislature,
But to the single autocratic feature
                      . . of government, —
The veto by . . Executive . . this . .
Something more imperial than republican.
Him they now think they can hold to . .
                         accountability.
(Him to — hymn to — Latinity.) —
The evils of Rome worked out
Thru ten centuries of barbarism.
History never *quite* repeats itself . .
No successful military leader
Will repeat in America
The threadbare experiences of Europe; —
The executive power is not likely to be seized
While the legislative is suppressed.
Indications rather point towards
Corruption of the legislative
And a quiet assumption of the executive.
To bring our vaunted institutions
Within the rule of all historic precedent . .
It, perhaps, only remains for the coming man
To carry the combination of elements
One step in advance, and put Caesarism

At once in control of the corporation and of the
proletariat.

1871.   Henry Adams.   My book is out ..
My own share in the volume .. less than half ..
And .. few works except possibly some few
Of Aristotle and Bacon contain anything
To compare with the wisdom of this .. vain
To expect proper appreciation in this world
And I have my doubts whether I shall fare
much better in any other ..
You will support .. my indifference .. to vulgar
opinion.

As one cannot doubt foreign press dispatches
Unless he wants to be expelled from the list
of civilized people,
Believe them and don't disturb me
in the other world,
"J. Stalin."

By means of this simple and smooth machinery,
Which differs in no essential respect from
roulette or rouge-et-noir ..
I went down to the neighborhood of Wall Street ..
And to my Newport steamer .. Mr. James
Fisk:
In blue uniform, broad gilt cap-band,
Three silver stars on coat-sleeve,
Lavender gloves, diamond breast-pin
Large as a cherry, stood at the gangway,
Surrounded by aides bestarred and bestriped
like myself ..
And welcomed President Ulysses Simpson Grant.

The Romans, after the Battle of Magnesia,
So far as the cities of the Western coast were concerned,
With a fresh outburst of coinage
Which in remembrance followed
The well-known types of Alexander.

1893. Brooks Adams.
Henry, like the good brother he was ..
Stayed with me in Quincy ..
I can see him .. as he used to stroll in the garden
                                        toward sunset.
"Please read this manuscript .. tell me
Whether it is worth printing
Or whether it is quite mad.
Probably there is nothing of value in it."
"The gold-bugs will never forgive you.
You are monkeying with a dynamo."
"I have no ambition to compete with Daniel Webster
As the jackal of the vested interests."

It will be remarked that these are matters of
Business in the strict sense.
Immaterial wealth.   Intangible assets.
As regards .. nature and origin ..
The outgrowth of three main lines of business-like
                                        management:
— limitation of supply with a view to profitable
                                        sales;
— obstruction of traffic with a view to profitable
                                        sales;
— meretricious publicity with a view to profitable
                                        sales.
A marketable right to get something for nothing.
They may even come high ..

If the cost to the community is taken into account ..
                                       (also)
The expenditure incurred by their owners for their
                                       upkeep.

"It is now full four generations since John Adams
Wrote the constitution of Massachusetts.
The world is tired of us
We have only survived because our ancestors
Lived in times of revolution."

Hot August .. and talked endlessly of panic.
If I live forever, I shall never forget
                        that summer.

1895.   "Dear Brooks:
"The nations, after a display of dreadful
Bad manners, are .. afraid to fight ..
Once more .. under the whip of the bankers.
Even on Cuba .. we are beaten and hopeless ..
Were we on the edge of a .. last great
                        centralization,
Or a first great movement of disintegration?
These are the facts on both sides ..
And this is what satiates my instinct for life ..
That our .. civilization .. has failed to
                        concentrate further.
Its next effort may succeed ..
With Russia .. the eccentric on one side and
                 America on the other .. "

1901.   Henry Adams.
Active, vibrating, mostly unconscious, and quickly
Reacting on force ..

(Brooks: men work unconsciously . .
   perform an act, before they can explain why;
      often centuries before)
Russia . . nothing in common . . with . .
Any . . world . . history knew;
She had been the oldest source
Of civilization in Europe, and
Had kept none for herself . .
Luminous . . salt of radium . .
But with . . negative luminosity
As though she were a substance whose
                energies had been sucked out —
. . Inert residuum — with movement of pure inertia.
— herders deserted by their leaders and herds.
— wandering waves stopped in their wanderings
— waiting for their winds or warriors to
   return and lead them westward;

Rhymes and rhymers pass away . .
The alien jumps the boat,
The sea reflected in mirrors.

tribes that had camped, like Khirgis, for
                        the season . .
had lost the means of motion without acquiring
               the habit of permanence.
They waited and suffered.
As they stood they were out of place . .
Their country . . sink of energy . .
The Caspian Sea . .
Its surface
Kept the uniformity of ice and snow.

From the first glimpse one caught

From the sleeping-car window,
In the early morning, of the
Polish Jew at the accidental railway station, in
All his .. horror,
To the last ..
Of the Russian peasant
Lighting his candle and
Kissing his ikon before
The railway Virgin in
The station at St. Petersburg ..

Dreary forests of Russia ..
Stockholm .. thru a New England landscape and
                              bright autumn ..
Discovered Norway
Triangulated .. vast surfaces of history ..
All his life against the beer-swilling
Saxon boors whom Freeman loved .. peering
At the flying tourist .. the lights of an electro-magnetic
                              civilization ..
The infinite seemed to have become loquacious:
An installation of electric lighting and telephones ..
Beyond the level of the magnetic pole ..
Look back across the gulf to Russia ..
The glacial ice-cap still pressed down ..
Dusky and oily sea ..
Ice-cap of Russian inertia ..

Nothing to say.
For him, all opinion founded on fact must be error,
Because the facts can never be complete,
And their relations must be always infinite.
Very likely, Russia, would instantly become —

Then feed, and be fat,

Come we to full points here; and are etceteras nothing?

Arrived mostly with bedding in a sheet
Samovar, with tall pitcher of pink glass,
With copper mugs, with a beard,
Without shaving mug —
To America's land of the pilgrim Jews?
To buy, after 20 years in a railroad flat,
A living room suite of varnished
Mahogany framed chairs and
Blue leather upholstery,
To be like everybody, with what
                              is about us.
And the youngest being born
                  here (in New York)
Always regretted having as a kid
Hit his brother's head with a shoe
In bed one bright Sunday morning.
Just like THAT, while his older brother
                              was still sleeping.
For no reason at all.
One phrase sticks in the head
"Love rests in Skeffington's." Memory's pulled
                                          windowshade:
Blind like Grasso in "Scuro" for three acts.
His older brother took him (the baby)
      to the theatre (mezzanine always)
Saturday matinee and night
And Sunday matinee and night.
Sunday you wished it were Friday.
Let *me* tell *you* about the state of Pennsylvania,
                              said Bob.

In Below the Grass Roots mine country

Of the "patch" smack on the culm
They bake pies such as you never ate.
Peter, blue-eyed, from the Russian steppes
Came here forty some years ago
And has since owned no other country
Pretty much as my allegiance
Owns no other pies.
The first time I approached the pit
A kid of sixteen
The colliery ambulance was already there —
A casualty, with the flesh hanging, coming out.
Well, I sit around waiting for the graveyard
          shift,
Not even fire-boss, and they've forgotten I hail
From William Penn —
And sometimes this splendid lion is invited to a meal,
I have my little chicken as tho she never had been real.
One kid gets the wish-bone and the
     other four each some wing,
The Mrs. just busy serving,
And Peter keeps the gizzard and the leg.
Even during Prohibition always a fluid dram.
Peter, take Oil and Burners, Inc.
They sell oil at 25¢ the gallon
Which costs them one-quarter cent to make,
At that it's a by-product, —
To public schools and churches
Which can use only this particular oil
For the particular burners
Oil and Burners sell to them.
"By golly, Bob, you know what I say
Criminal, divide 'em up!"
Well if you just don't all see alike
And some one guy sees a little more

Than is good for all
We all just can't win.
"By golly, Bob, come some slob
                    make that happen
Divide 'em up again!"

Wherever I sit
Is the head of the table. Not too
Near Spinoza refusing a new coat:
It would be a bad situation
If the bag were better than the meat in it.

Said Albert — where? — in infinite diapers:
The bitter and sweet come from the outside,
The hard from one's own efforts.
For the most part, I do the thing which my
                    own nature
Drives me to do.
It is shameful to earn so much respect
                    and love for it.
I live in that singleness painful in youth,
   but delicious in the years of maturity.

1935.   Eight thousand
Men, operators,
Set themselves above the law
Not enough food, clothing and
Shelter in the hard coal land
To keep the wolf from the door.
                    Nineteen

Thirty-five, knowing the coal was stolen
From us, we workers will use our
Organized strength in this fight to dig coal.

10% of Pennsylvania's anthracite's ours, 19-
35.

Go splintered rondel as a nosegay to Bob
And tip off his friends, who retrieve
The state of Pennsylvania
Like the present governor of that State,
Hasn't he said:
I wasn't *their* candidate ..
Suppose I were to grant their request
And send State troopers in there.
It would take 2,000 men and cost
The State $14,000 a day.
When they were withdrawn
If unemployment continued,
The bootlegging would start all over again.
The coal operators .. brought these people
Into the .. region,
Let them build homes and churches ..
Then closed down the mines
To concentrate their operations
So that they could make bigger profits ..
Made millions from the labor of these men .. now
Unemployed. They can't let them starve,
Or go out of that State —
To Police Sergeant Jasper McKinney —
Who most probably will never read a line of verse
And who most likely never having been to Egypt
Was "never made blind by mummy dust" —
Handling some notes warning "lay off that union,"
Commented: "I believe this
Was the work of anti-union men
Who left the notes
To throw us off the track."

Go where (not from the cemetery) —
Not as once to the Argentine,
The competition's too keen.
Go where (not alive on the running-board) —
Trappings rise —
No bridges, no breeches, not after midnight.
Go (as quick as the news-print turns yellow) as
The Araucanian Indians' sacred tree Canelo
Shipped from Chile to the U. S. A.
And back again to Chile:
After the khaki inspectors of the American
                              Department of Agriculture
Peered six month at the plant, it withered
To a few dusty stalks
In Washington's Indian summer, District of Columbia.
Go with the ghost's arm of a dead friend
                              in a coat sleeve,
Spring rain on his face —
Who had picked snails and made chowder,
Dark hair gilding from the sea chlorine,
The salt evaporating on the body in small crystals.
Leg casts of sand on the ghost,
Tinker with machines
After pressing comfortably upside down on your groin
                              in the dunes —

A voice craves perfection:
        'our age in our wrists
            use 'em for levers'.

Wrestling with body smell —
Sunset — green waves — the meadow lark
                at the bayberry's end —
Spray of the Atlantic dashed in
                the mouth.

With our most valuable capital,
With labor's arterial blood,
Tailor,
Enlevez-moi quelques kilomètres d'ici —
Voiced after "Ulysses", perhaps before the invention of
stream-line.
I am lost in these trousers
And empire.

How many men must we kill —
As fast as you can breed them, O mothers!
The Great Boot, fathers of Italia, pinches:
You must never have peace
Out of your trousers!
Fascisti, you must never have time
To mate out of your trousers!

Herr Führer und Heiland,
Es jüdelt der Judenbaum!
Es geht hier her wie in einer Judenschule
(Sic, madhouse) in Deutchland. Swines grubbing
hate in their speech:
Haust du meinen Juden, hau' ich deinen Juden,
As when a lady says "juice" for Jews.

Thou'rt an Emperor, Caesar, Keiser and Pheezar:
Froth and lime —
O base Hungarian wight! wilt thou the spigot wield?

Which of you know Ford of this town?
He hath a legion of angels.

Then did the sun on dunghill shine.

With wit or steel?

We offered peace to the nations
At a time when our offer
Could be taken for weakness.
We repeat it now, our armed forces
Stronger than any possible enemy
Or any possible alliance of enemies.

For labor who will sing —
The cultured growth is scrapped,
The retarding, the prevailing.
Tomb of song — of this, perhaps, final Xmas —
Cracked who could render the Greek —
Five continents arm for war.

Anchor a little way out —
You are not the most favored nation.
The seamen are striking, will the longshoremen
                                come out for the shape-up?

Preventives for this ease?
Friends, let two fingers salute.
If these banks' moneys come out of nothing
And take out of all
Will No Thing — No Man —
Resign to the people's issue of nothing,
Or must he devolve upon all?

By what name you call your people
Whether by that of freemen or of slaves ..
That in some countries
The *laboring* poor were called freemen,

In others slaves ..
Workers producing a surplus:
John Adams — to distract minds?
Boost figures to a gross of red revolutions:
All less costly than wars.
It is not by the consolidation
Or concentration of powers (corporate bodies)
But by their distribution,
That good government is effected.

Nor should we wonder at .. pressure
When we consider the monstrous abuses
Under which .. people were ground to powder.

Cite .. Sight ..
The body
            lies awake sitting,
Bodies step over their own bodies.

Cite,
John Adams or cite Lenin:
I thought of workers and peasants;
It's good nobody hears
Your national, psychological hypothesis
Or someone might say
'The old man is flattered by country'.

Workers and farmers are no Roman mob.
They are not maintained by the State,
They maintain the State by their work.

Things move forward so slowly,

World history does not seem to hurry,
But I tell you frankly, myself
I am little impressed by your 'center'
Which does not understand, which has
No energy to have done with petty demagogues.

Untiring action, but free
From the lie that it can take the place
                              of mass action.
We are not Xerxes who had the sea
                        scourged with chains.
But to determine the facts does not
                        mean to give up the struggle.
Learn, learn, learn!
Act, act, act!
Be prepared, well and completely prepared
To make use, with all our forces,
Of the next revolutionary wave.
That is our job.

Good day,
The 'left' really
Thinks, the International is a faithful Penelope.
Well, our International does not weave
                              during the day
To undo its work during the night. —
Thanks for such Marxism
Which immediately attributes all society
To its economic basis.

And I mistrust the sexual theories of the articles,
                        dissertations, pamphlets . .
In short, that . . literature which
Flourishes in the dirty soil of society.

I mistrust those who are always contemplating
The several questions, like the Indian saint his
                              navel ..
Arbitrary hypotheses .. personal need
To justify personal abnormality .. before
Middle-class morality, and to entreat its patience.

Everything has its time ..
And this moment's more urgent than incest.
The little yellow-beaked birds who have just
                              broken
From the egg of ideas are so frightfully
                              clever.

This is the battle:
Her hair shall have what color it pleases,
A style superfluous as breath,
The pulse of light be timed to
The speed of the film
Which moves past the lens' pinhole
At velocities up to 200 miles an hour,
The sun fire again in the cells of the animal,
The picture of a drop at superspeed
Roll off glass as a perfect crown.

My kinsman knows:
The bastard killed his dog,
The cross-eyed bastard just
Calmly drove over him;
A head can heave out of a palm
And love be an 8 in a precise walk;
A jacket for swimmer's shoulders,
The horse boy's blue eyes in Greek marble —
                    "New York, N.Y.

Editor, Times Union:
   I would die for dear old Standard Oil
                Ex-Soldier,
                  12:47 P. M.''

This water you almost got killed for,
Said David, do you expect me to drink it?

Marx to his daughter Jenny:
It is dull since you went away —
Without you and Jenny and Harra and Mr. Tea.
The day before yesterday the Dogberry Club was here ..
I don't dislike the wife .. she has a brusque,
Unconventional and decided way of thinking
                         and speaking,
But it is funny to see how admiringly
Her eyes fasten upon the lips
Of her self-satisfied garrulous husband. —
The breast in the mental planking. —
Company .. can't well live altogether without it,
And that when you get it ..
You try hard to rid yourself of ..

Writing its signature different each time, so
you cannot get your money back.

This matter is the substratum of all
   Changes going on in the world.

To the Impossible, marriage to no less —
No sleeper beside,
By side instrument unstrung

March arms entwined into the fields,
Green, grass and eyelashes,
They sign well voices under the rays —
The smoke streaks lulling over motors.

What did the mule say when the tidal wave
                                        came
And the new religion was born as he
                                sat down?
He asked, "The Future of Literature:
                Will It Be A Sport? —
Literature is an *art* based on the *abuse* of
                                    language
It is based on *language* as a creator
                            of illusions.."

Académicien and poet squinting cat eyes,
Pick of the State's forget-me-nots,
Who stinks up the "Flowers" you devise
While you wreathe a future made by snots? —

O little nanny-goat daddy bought for two cents
Who reviewed whose tiny metal warriors?
Général Gene Gem mobilized and reviewed
                At the Invalides
A parade of 80,000 tiny metal warriors to-day.
They are the collection
Of the Society of the Collectors of Tin Soldiers,
Membership of which includes F. B. K.,
Former Secretary of State of the U. S. A.
                Paris, 7 juin, last year,
                        (AP).

China, the one place it could happen:

"Most honorable Sir,
                    We perused your MS.
with boundless delight. And
we hurry to swear by our ancestors
we have never read any other
that equals its mastery.
Were we to publish your work,
we could never presume again on
our public and name
to print books of a standard
not up to yours.
For we cannot imagine
that the next ten thousand years
will offer its ectype.
We must therefore refuse
your work that shines as it were in the sky
and beg you a thousand times
to pardon our fault
which impairs but our own offices.
                    — , Publishers".

Toba Harbor, Japan, Oct. 1936. —
Kokichi Mikimoto is content.
The Japanese pearl king.
Who rose from the humble station of noodle peddler
To the exalted one of merchant prince,
Prepared for the beyond yesterday
With these ceremonies:
    A memorial service for the "souls"
Of hundreds of millions of oysters
That had been "martyred" to make Mr. Mikimoto a
                                        fortune.

    A rehearsal of Mr. Mikimoto's own funeral
                                service.

Jodo priests prayed and chanted
For the oysters "slaughtered" over a period of thirty
years.

Mr, Mikimoto and 42 members of his family
Attended the premature funeral.

And this not for the newspapers:
November of F. D. R.'s second election —
The trolley goes across town
From where was once the village of West Farms,
And midway you get off; a short walk to 1229
Washington Ave.,
Thomas Hicks, General Blacksmith and Tool Maker.
Borough of The Bronx, and this district in the
nineteenth century
The Township of Morrisania
Where a century before that, on the waters of,
They wanted to build the capital of the United
States of America.
His sign-board over the shop, a shed
    with a front of glass panes:
Peered — saw twilight inside,
That and early evening lamplight
On the high ceiling, in the dust of some tools, —
Before climbing one flight up wood stairs
Past the old door, oak or what, heavy to push.
The long second after the knock — "Mr. Hicks?"
"Come in." A draft.   Darkness,
But for the flame of the belly-stove.
And you did not see Russia in the green-blue
light of the coal,
Could faster see Lady Greensleeves
quick now as fayërye;
"You bet", to you

As his guest
From his father and his grandfather
Who had left the North — this borough here —
                        for the West,
And from himself who'd come back from the West
                                to the East.
Drooping mustaches, which had been red, gray
                        under the rheum;
Thru a cold
Asked you to sit down in the patchwork quilt,
The national tapestry,
And asked your friend of eight years standing
                        also to sit
In the quilt,
For the bed sank in the dark.
Thomas Hicks saving on light,
Informing the researchist in old gardens
                        (for $ 23.86 a week —
'Why and 86 cents, why not $ 24,' Telemachus
                                had asked):
The gas station on Hicks' corner
Had some time ago fumed out his garden.
But could he pencil a sketch of it,
Or draw a plan
— (The old battlefield in one corner,
Old Glory rolled up on its staff
As thick as you could guess his wrist had been) — ?

"Hicks lived in Jim De Lancey's house, West Farms Rd.
Jim De Lancey became so poor, he worked as a farmer
On Thomas Powell's land. Powell had bought De
                                Lancey's plots.
Hicks bought off Cambrellion connected with the

Then there is the story of John B. Haskins,
                        Congressman,
Who owned all Woodlawn Cemetery,
And the check the tax-bureau had to
Accept from him after they'd refused it.
Out of a clear sky one year they decided to
                        raise the tax rate.
Haskins hadn't set up a stick on his land.
When he got his check back in the mail
He put it right back in his pocket —
And said, if you can prove the ground
'S worth more with the few recent corpses
I'll drop in and see you,
Otherwise come up and see me.
My father who told this story, I was there
At the time, may have taken bets on Jerome Racetrack,
I beg your pardon" (for manhandling your
                        coat's lapels)
"But I never did see him other than sober.
New steel or New Deal or Steal,
If the common man get together — "
The Manifesto?
Or maybe as F. D. R., diverted at a
            dinner the year after,
Would jest,
The invested Ambassador to Maine?

Plenty of eloquence,
Words enough,
Such hardened soldiers of fortune who became softies,
How could they escape
When the canals of the ear relate the head

             to the wood-grain of a chair.
Enough and more than enough,
My father would not have any one curse
             in his home,
Would say, we too, once were made delectable
             by the pipes of the organ,
Heaven of Substance, penetrant music,
Sub-cherubim of the air —
Above colonnade wake forms.

Devotions that made the waste pits lie deep,
Atonement's prayer at sundown full of fissures.

And history: in Shanghai,
A woman's base swung into motion,
Her arms played croquet,
A Chinese stuck in barbed wire;
Never wanting to sweep gold off the street —
Behind chicken coops,
Looms so close together, operators
Could barely stand up to work between them;
Fifty good reasons in that overcoat
Why he could not go back to Marked Tree —
Fifty holes from the guns of vigilantes,
Negroes and whites holding the doors
             against night-riders.

Fires in moving kitchens,
The first minstrel warbles "turkey in the straw".
Flood.   Cave in.
Prostrate.
Waving grain, goats' hair.
Civil wars: steel helmet and flashlight blue.

Nazis lured by *super-Nazis* —

"Become super-Nazis" in order the more quickly
To destroy the régime by its own excesses.

"I have led my ragamuffins where they are peppered"

1937. "White Moors" — Germans — against Germans
Fighting for each street of Madrid of the UNITED
                                                    FRONT.

More than one civil war:
"Madrid will be Fascism's Tomb",
Evening, a voice shouts in perfect Italian:
"Come on, you pigs of Italians!   Come on!"

Some plane's bombs don't explode,
"Friendly fliers in enemy bombers that search
                                with their flares?"

Randolfo Pacciardi and Umberto Galliani, and Pietro
                                                    Nenni,
Former close friend of Il Duce, in the
                                International Column.

Kiss all the little ones for me ..
So cold .. the freezing of the ink on .. my pen
Renders it difficult to write ..
The Batture at New Orleans.
The proceedings of the Government of the United
                                                    States
In maintaining the Public Right to the Beach of
                                the Mississippi,
Adjacent to New Orleans,
Against Intrusion of Edward Livingston.

Prepared for the Use of Counsel, by Thos. Jefferson.
Livingston (the waters used to run his saw mills),
                         27 June 1809:
"Congress will probably adjourn
Without coming to any decision
On the subject of my removal by the late president
                         of the United States
From my estate at New Orleans."
A most ungrateful complaint; for had he not
Been removed, he must, at the time of writing
                         this letter,
Have been, as his estate was,
Some 10 or 12 feet under water,
The river being then at its greatest height.
.. without appeal to learned authorities,
does not common sense,
the foundation of all authorities of the laws
                         themselves ..
Let him be consumed .. !

1821 .. for my own more ready reference,
.. for the information of my family ..
some recollections of dates and facts
concerning myself ..
the destinies of my life ..

science ..
          in which things are placed ..

.. interested in considering British claims
as a common cause to all ..
and to produce a unity of action ..
with the help of Rushworth,
whom we rummaged over

for the revolutionary precedents
and forms of the Puritans of that day,
preserved by him,
we cooked up a resolution,
somewhat modernizing their phrases ..
prayer .. to avert the evils of civil war ..
to inspire us .. in support of our rights ..

(Like *Bloody Sunday* in St. Petersburg!)

But a half page further:
This was in May ..
And the effect of the day was like a shock
of electricity ..

(I imagine that this elastic fluid
Is more and more dense
As it approaches the surface of bodies
And for some distances within them,
As is likewise observed
In the air surrounding the earth.
Cadwallader Colden).

.. arousing every man .. placing him erect ..
solidly on his center ..

bringing together facts
which appearances separate:
all that is created in a fact
is the language that numbers it,
The facts clear,
breath lives
with the image each lights.

"The houses and trees stand where they did ..

the flowers come forth ..
reproducing their like ..
The hyacinths and tulips ..
the irises giving place to ..
as your mama has .. to you,
my dear Anne,   '
as you will to the sisters of ..
and as I shall .. to you all ..
wishing you .. good night.
                   Thomas Jefferson."

.. moving matter, bodies.
The eye corrects the inch,
when workers and even manufacturers
and merchants
understand my book ..

What is music which does not
In any sense progress?
Great improvement of the sense
          of hearing.
Concordant old as good as good
        Discordant new:
"So made that all the parts together,
Or either severally .. may be sung" —
Resolved like Simone Molinare
          (Miller)
Against the Mill of time, purveyor
Of the earth's hope, with canorous pearls
In the shell of beauty, and with beams like Venus
             To the sun.

A pretty May note,
Singing Bach as they dug,

Isenacum en musica, hear us
Digging — we are singing of gardens — March
Day of equal night, Bach's *chorus primus*
To *chorus secundus* to the groined arch —
To vanish as the cone fruit of the larch:
Voice a voice blown, returning as May, dew
On night grass: and he said I worked hard, hue
Of word on the melody, (each note worth
Thought the clatter of a water-mill drew):
Labor, light lights in air, on earth, in earth.

May is, Airs wreathe (times) : and they mirror: plus
Silence supports my pretension .. the parts
Ascend a tone, repeating, (tin ears) thus
(Listen) move past Jesus ratted in starch;
My contention .. that the slight disregards
My costs: Recorders: *Fa* — as what wind blew
Tossed coins in herrings heads, what journey thru
Mi et Mi Fa .. tota Musica, dearth
Such as voice courting voice has such value
Labor light lights in air, in earth, on earth:

(Times): that dug under the set hymns, *tonus
Contrarius* — .. Lags a new May discards:
Old chant, flaked arch, for live contrapunctus;
Plays till four notes give out their names: old Bach's
Here: blind .. — hands (birds wing fall digging).

                                                         Son .. shard
Where orchards were .. has two boys .. the May view
Tunneled heap of ruin. Shirt rags imbue
A red, free blood, Men, Men of Madrid, girth
Of the attacker dogs will not stop you

Labor, light lights in air, on earth, in earth.

Coda, see to it the burden renew,
Sound out thick gardens dug up in purlieu
The shrapnel haunts; May is red blossom, berth
Of what times' mill; blood reads the wounds, the cue —
Luteclavicembalo — bullets pursue:
Labor light lights in earth, in air, on earth.

9

An impulse to action sings of a semblance
Of things related as equated values,
The measure all use is time congealed labor
In which abstraction things keep no resemblance
To goods created; integrated all hues
Hide their natural use to one or one's neighbor.
So that were the things words they could say: Light is
Like night is like us when we meet our mentors
Use hardly enters into their exchanges,
Bought to be sold things, our value arranges;
We flee people who made us as a right is
Whose sight is quick to choose us as frequenters,
But see our centers do not show the changes
Of human labor our value estranges.

Values in series taking on as real
We affect ready gold a steady token
Flows in unbroken circuit and induces
Our being, wearies of us as ideal
Equals that heady crises eddy. Broken
Mentors, unspoken wealth labor produces,
Now loom as causes disposing our loci,
The foci of production: things reflected
As wills subjected; formed in the division
Of labor, labor takes on our imprecision —
Bought, induced by gold at no gain, though close eye
And gross sigh fixed upon gain have effected
Value erected on labor, prevision

Of surplus value, disparate decision.

Hands, heart, not value made us, and of any
Desired perfection the projection solely,
Lives worked us slowly to delight the senses,
Of their fire shall you find us, of the many
Acts of direction not defection — wholly
Dead labor, lowlier with time's offenses,
Assumed things of labor powers extorted
So thwarted we are together impeded —
The labor speeded while our worth decreases —
Naturally surplus value increases
Being incident to the pace exhorted:
Unsorted, indrawn, but things that time ceded
To life exceeded — not change, the mind pieces
The expanse of labor in us when it ceases.

Light acts beyond the phase day wills us into
Call a maturer day, the poor are torn — a
Pawl to adorn a ratchet — hope dim — eying
Move cangues, conjoined the coils of things they thin to,
With allayed furor the obscurer bourne, a
Stopped hope unworn, a voiced look, mask espying
That, as things, men want in us yet behoove us,
Disprove us least as things of light appearing
To the will gearing to light's infinite locus:
Not today but tomorrow is their focus.
No one really knows us who does not prove us,
None or times move us but that we wake searing
The labor veering from guises which cloak us,
As animate instruments men invoke us.

Dissemble — pledging complexions so guarded —
Cast of plied error leaves such error asserted
But stand obverted, men sight us things joined to
Change itself edging the full light discarded —
In machines' terror a use there averted —
Times have subverted the plenty they point to:
Things, we have not always known this division —
Misprision of interest, profit, rent — coded
Surplus, decoded as labor — evaded
As gain the source of all wealth so degraded
The land and the worker elude the vision —
A scission of surplus aud use corroded
And still, things goaded by labor, nor faded,
But like light in which its action was aided.

We are things, say, like a quantum of action
Defined product of energy and time, now
In these words which rhyme now how song's exaction
Forces abstraction to turn from equated
Values to labor we have approximated.

An eye to action sees love bear the semblance
Of things, related is equated, — values
The measure all use who conceive love, labor
Men see, abstraction they feel, the resemblance
(Part, self-created, integrated) all hues
Show to natural use, like Benedict's neighbor
Crying his hall's flown into the bird: Light is
The night isolated by stars (poled mentors)
Blossom eyelet enters pealing with such changes
As sweet alyssum, that not-madness, (ranges
In itself, there tho acting without right) is —

Whose sight is rays, "I shall go; the frequenters
That search our centers, love; Elysium exchanges
No desires; its thought loves what hope estranges."

Such need may see reason, the perfect real —
A body ready as love's steady token
Fed thought unbroken as pleasure induces —
True to thought wearies never its ideal
That loves love, head, every eddy. Broken
Plea, best unspoken, a lip's change produces
Suffers to confuse this thought and its loci,
The foci of things timelessly reflected —
Substance subjected to no human prevision,
Free as exists it loves: worms dig; imprecision
Of indignation cannot make the rose high
Or close sigh, therein blessedness effected
Thru power has directed love to envision
Where body is it bears a like decision.

Virtue flames value, merriment love — any
Compassed perfection a projection solely
Power, the lowly do not tune the senses;
More apt, more salutary body moves many
Minds whose direction makes defection wholly
Vague. This sole lee is love: from it offences
To self or others die, and the extorted
Word, thwarted dream with eyes open; impeded
Not by things seeded from which strength increases;
Remindful of its deaths as loves decreases;
Happy with the dandelion unsorted,
Well-sorted by imagination speeded
To it, exceeded night lasts, the sun pieces

Its necessary nature, error ceases.

Love acts beyond the phase day wills it into —
Hate is obscure, errs, is pain, furor, torn — a
Lust to adorn aversion, hope — love eying
Its object joined to its cause, sees path into
Things the future or now, that poorer bourne, a
Past, a step, a worn, a voiced look, gone — eying
These, each in itself is saying, "behoove us,
Disprove us least as things of love appearing
In a wish gearing to light's infinite locus,
Balm or jewelweed is according to focus.
No one really knows us who does not love us,
Time does not move us, we are and love, searing
Remembrance — veering from guises which cloak us,
So defined as eternal, men invoke us."

A wise man pledging piety unguarded
Lives good not error. By love's heir are asserted
Song, light obverted to mind, joy enjoined to
Least death, act edging patience, envy discarded;
Difficult rare excellence, love's heir, averted
Loss seize the hurt head Apollo's eyes point to:
Ai, *Ai* Hyacinthus, the petals in vision —
The scission living acquiescence, coded
Tempers decoded for friendship, evaded
Image recurring to vigilance, raided
By falsehood burning it clear to the vision,
Derision transmuted by laughter, goaded
Voice holding the node at heart, song, unfaded
Understanding whereby action is aided.

Love speaks: "in wracked cities there is less action,

Sweet alyssum sometimes is not of time; now
Weep, love's heir, rhyme now how song's exaction
Is your distraction — related is equated,
How else is love's distance approximated."

10

Paris
Paris
Of your beautiful phrases
Is fallen
The wire service halted

Go ahead Paris
London tunes in the Nazi broadcast already on
New York feels the raid over Tours
                    in the noon-hour cafés
Cannot hear Paris
Come over the air

Stares as into a bomb crater
At all the announcements
Of baseball scores that matter
Or do not matter a damn
The song passed out of the voices
As freedom goes out of speech

All the people of Paris
Mass, massed refugees on the roads
Go to mass with the air
            and the shrapnel for a church
A Christian civilization
Where Pius blesses the black-shirts

Kyrie

Kyrie eleison
They sang
The song passes out of the voices
                    one whisper

Cry louder
People   people   people
Alone each one is a whisper
A mess sucked out
No substance

Cry out in the streets of New York
But cry out in the streets of London
Cry loudest in the streets of Paris

People   people   people
There is no whisper but vibrates
Your body
No voice alone but that *you*
Speak it

Poor songster so weak
Stopped singing to curse
A mess sucked out
No substance

People   people
But you record it
                    Christ!

Glory on high
            and in earth peace

Battered France halts her railroads

To freeze the flight south of her millions
From the Germans still advancing

Return   return
Men women children of France
                    ten million
Troop back to your occupied north
Your government free to choose its seat
Even occupied Paris
Be interned, the enemy permits the government
To hold you in Paris
Wireless in all France forbidden
It's no betrayal when your newspapers report
The British radio calls to you in French
                              to help France
Henri Philippe Pétain and Herr Hitler
                    have made peace
One name is spit
The other is hawked from the throat

French people, Spain's dead asked you to help
Now you cannot ask them for help
Do you still ask us gullible people for help
Stop crying for France, snarls Italy
What more could they have done
   to merit our heel in their necks?

French people
Mercy is in your arms
Against invaders
And commanders who gave up the defense!
You held Sedan, your generals
         unpinned that hinge
Your eyes have mercy

To see betrayer and invader wiped out.

Frenchmen resist   flee to Britain
Proclaim indissoluble union
        of your two peoples
Of peoples
Let the English seize your ships
Such acts are holy, Britons
And uproot, hide the parks about London
Tear up heaths scar the earth
Paint the roofs of your homes with trees
Hide for your defense
Nightingales lively this spring

You common people in the blackout

Children hidden separated out

One son delights
To lie awake listening —

To your defense!
British people!
If any of the few thousand Alpine Chasseurs
Who held out in the Jura
Saved 300,000 of the men of France
Only to see them betrayed
If any French Alpine Chasseurs, Britons
Escaped to the bombed shores of England
Fit them out with your planes like your own
Let them bomb
German France.

As the sons of your two peoples

Fought Franco together
In the International Column in Spain

Credo   I believe

          Shame

Ashamed of all people put to shame
And all planets emit light
     and indeed all bodies do

China Ethiopia Spain Austria
Czechoslovakia Albania Poland
Denmark Norway Holland
Belgium Luxemburg France
One substance visible and
                         invisible
Decay
The death of millions visible
     Corpus
Of the trade of arms
The profits of oil
A vicar of Christ sworn to traitors
His priests who thrive on silver
More ashamed beaten to sleep beside lashed Jews
Than to abet murder
In all countries at war
     or not yet at war
The depraved fearing for their estates
The old betrayers, corrugate patriots
        "For Labor, Family and Country"
Under their breaths
          Slavery Penury Ruin
Harrowing workers

Till the country has no defense
Driving both aliens and citizens under dive bombers
Herding peasants into firing onslaught of tanks
Plotting plebiscites migrations
Hunger for all but themselves
Moving entire cities to certain death
Shadowing lives everywhere
   with spies, laws, tests, and the last mark,
      final zero of death

       Incarnate
Carcass smiles
Corpses block the bridges
Machine gun outposts smell of
Dead gunners piled sandbags now
Exported here the Japanese textile girls
       will have nothing to gain
No more than at home have the geishas
For rivers to flow with brandy
Peace is ruptured

No slant-eyed devil on stilts
Drunk the Japanese invader fights
       Brothers Chinese
Rising Sun roosts also at home
Night dawn noon evening
Chinese murder Chinese
French and British concessioners consort
     with Japanese greed
Betrayals bankers' wars from across seas
To gain the scorched earth of China

The Eighth Route People's Army
Holding

Holding out in a seven thousand mile retreat
Populace piled into brushwood burnt alive
Driven up forested mountain tops
Set afire from below go into earth

And the Japanese into the earth

Cowardice swells its new Axis

Mussolini's mouth over the people of Italy
Hoarse throat of the German Reich
Rasp on the free body of Spain
With their aim London
With their aim Paris
With their aim the United States
With their aim The International Brigade

Spain
The first sample of lightning attack
Victim of world centers looking away
Four columns of the enemy converged on Madrid
One column of the enemy
Blistered inside
Teruel Guernica churr into earth
In Barcelona the bombs heavier than
            ever in war
Craters of earth
Three raids by seaplanes an hour flared
            by incendiary bombs
Spain remembered by the words
            The Fifth Column
The snake sliced still moves
Spain after two years levelled to earth

The snake
Rings communications
  shames birds
Sucks loyal men eggs
Anti-semites in Italy once
 people scarcely civilized hostile to Jews
In Berlin "clear street" is the signal to loot
The tailor's dummy hat on
Hangs with a rope around its neck

Prague
Overnight the new phrase

Forbidden to telephone
To telegraph
To transact —
Confiscated.

Germany, caterpillars
Crawl with ideals of endless chains
Feet trap all
Air traps all
So the Czechs can go back to the Reich
So the Esthonian Baltic Germans
 will come back into German earth
  for all time out of memory
And the Pole go into the earth
The Jew into middle Europe's rivers
Like a stone to the Holy Land for England
   to ship back to the Reich
The Danes to melt like their butter
The Norwegians into German arms
Rotterdam into the earth
Never such mass death as in Rotterdam

Not thru Belgium can the
    hunted shake off the smell
Not on Switzerland's borders
Not in Paris saved for the Reich

The Giver of life makes the dying come
There's nothing like it
To the bombed districts under the
    stringed lights of the bombers
Their super-sights
From which nations are running
All resemblance to what lives or is dead
    coincident with thoughts not waiting for tears
Let a better time say
The poet stopped singing to talk

He can shoot
Who could not take life

He will hunt the Rhino
           Before death

The Rhino is a lovely beast
He has two horns or one at least
And neither horn is just a horn
Provoking a dictator's scorn
His surest backside venting scorn
He sits upon the Rhino's horn
And corporate spumes up a yeast
The Rhino such a lovely beast

Empaled beneath the Rhino's knee
People foul in its wet majesty

It feels them with a heavy paw
The spittle dribbles from its jaw
He mires their bleeding overalls
The loveliest of animals

Love moved to earth cannot agree
                              with death
Nor as you know Molotov
Can treaties last an age
With the conquering Idea
            unconquered.

            Holy
Holy is Sylvie
        A little girl
Paul and Hélène's daughter
        It is her name
        She said in French
        "Le jour est déjà fini
        C'est la nuit qui tombe
        Et les poupettes
            qui attrapent froid
        On les enterre
        Et on leur chante"

        And in English
        "Day is over now
        It is night that falls
        And the dolls
            who take cold
        We bury them
        And sing to them"

There is a port in Canada
    called Ferry End
Glasses clink
Ale is the language
"La fenêtre" offers the British tar treating
"O. K.!" agrees the French sailor
"La fenêtre?" solicits the Briton
Considering both glasses
The *matelot* raises his empty, "O. K.!"

Lord   earth is full of Sylvie's glory.

We border on Canada
Nothing there but by labor
Or the Indian will wait till he
                digs us up.

      Go ahead Paris
There'll be famine next winter

"Why not kill Eugene's rabbit
    and serve it for supper?"
Eugene, 12, hears
His body hangs from a belt
Around his neck and the stair railing

Sun and a bird busy —
Between shutter and blind
Yellow thread

The Lady from the countryside
Has no carriage in which to ride
No, not a horse
She doesn't run of course

The child hiding
Against the wall
Steals an egg
He wants to fry it
He can't diet
On a knife

The capital of France is Vichy

Blessed is the new age-old effervescence

Till the sailors who mistook their planet
                              for a light
And took the wrong soundings
Come back

And the people
Grant us the people's peace.

11

for Celia and Paul

River that must turn full after I stop dying
Song, my song, raise grief to music
Light as my loves' thought, the few sick
So sick of wrangling: thus weeping,
Sounds of light, stay in her keeping
And my son's face — this much for honor.

Freed by their praises who make honor dearer
Whose losses show them rich and you no poorer
Take care, song, that what stars' imprint you mirror
Grazes their tears; draw speech from their nature or
Love in you — faced to your outer stars — purer
Gold than tongues make without feeling
Art new, hurt old: revealing
The slackened bow as the stinging
Animal dies, thread gold stringing
The fingerboard pressed in my honor.

Honor, song, sang the blest is delight knowing
We overcome ills by love. Hurt, song, nourish
Eyes, think most of whom you hurt. For the flowing
River 's poison where what rod blossoms. Flourish
By love's sweet lights and sing *in them I flourish.*
No, song, not any one power
May recall or forget, our
Love to see your love flows into

Us. If Venus lights, your words spin, to
Live our desires lead us to honor.

Graced, your heart in nothing less than in death, go —
I, dust — raise the great hem of the extended
World that nothing can leave; having had breath go
Face my son, say: 'If your father offended
You with mute wisdom, my words have not ended
His second paradise where
His love was in her eyes where
They turn, quick for you two — sick
Or gone cannot make music
You set less than all.   Honor

His voice in me, the river's turn that finds the
Grace in you, four notes first too full for talk, leaf
Lighting stem, stems bound to the branch that binds
                                              the
Tree, and then as from the same root we talk, leaf
After leaf of your mind's music, page, walk leaf
Over leaf of his thought, sounding
His happiness: song sounding
The grace that comes from knowing
Things, her love our own showing
Her love in all her honor.'

12

Out of deep need
Four trombones and the organ in the nave
A torch surged —
Timed the theme Bach's name,
Dark, larch and ridge, night:
From my body to other bodies
Angels and bastards interchangeably
Who had better sing and tell stories
Before all will be abstracted.
So goes: first, *shape*
The creation —
A mist from the earth,
The whole face of the ground;
Then *rhythm* —
And breathed breath of life;
Then *style* —
That from the eye its function takes —
"Taste" we say — a living soul.
First, glyph; then syllabary,
Then letters.   Ratio after
Eyes, tale in sound. First, dance.   Then
Voice. First, body — to be seen and to pulse
Happening together.
Before the void there was neither
Being nor non-being;
Desire, came warmth,
Or which, first?
Until the sages looked in their hearts

For the kinship of what is in what is not.
   Or in the heart or in the head?
      Quire after over three millenia.

A year, a month and 19 days before —
   the void in effect —

Sense sure, else not motion,
Madness to ecstasy never so thralled
But showed some quantity of choice
Eyes without feeling, feeling without sight
Ears without hands or eyes, smelling sans all
Or but a sickly part of one true sense
Could not so mope

Who tells time on all fours, yet moves
Shape, love —

         sense and openhandedness

    Blest
    Ardent   good,
    Celia,   speak simply, rarely   scarce, seldom —
    Happy, immeasurable love
      heart or head's greater part unhurt and happy,
      things that bear harmony
      certain in concord with reason.

From the spring of *Art of Fugue:*
The parts of a fugue should behave like reasonable men
  in an orderly discussion

From the source of *A Midsummer-Night's Dream:*

How comes this gentle concord in the world?

The order that rules music, the same
   controls the placing of the stars and the feathers
   in a bird's wing.
In the middle of harmony
Most heavenly music
For the universe is true enough.

Four horses like four notes.

Have your odyssey
How many voiced it be
"Speak to me in a different anguish

      It's a bee-star — no!
         a bumble-bee star — it's
         a star!"   A flying seeded
         dandelion, a something — a jack
         a star-feather — and Paul looks
         as if it might sting him
         as
         it floats away into the grass.
         To the day: a month before he was five.

            I would like to
            have a happy

Paul   Louis
from
his
nice best best
friend of Louis

Valentine's day because
there are no hearts. There
will be a heart because
we will send you a letter
that was from me to
divide it in half.

Take and owe nothing.
Everybody take. Here,
And owe nothing.
How else can we permit
That word, cobbler,
What else is *beauty's* last?

Without the mask!
Why do you flee our torches
Made out of the wood of trees
The prophets bewept and intoned?
I am different, let not a gloss embroil you.

From the spring recalled:

Unfinished is against the laws of the *spirit*.
Take that word I never use — no word someone
can't use.

Well-tempered forces count:
As the preludio of the Third Partita dances,
As the countersubject of the fourfold 19th fugue
Signed on death lightly,
B, A, C, H,
Stopped here
With the last Choral-Prelude
Told his son-in-law Altnikol.
The violinist phrases — as Bach wished? —
From the thought of the somewhat slackened bow:
Music does not always
Call on the human voice
Only free (often wordless)
Men are grateful to one another.

Voice without scurf or gray matter,
For the eyes of the mind are proofs.

A closed missal in a flood
For posterity
  To Celia
Comes from who thinks
He can say modestly
To everybody,
While you're partly right you're all wrong —
I speak to myself most often.
If each time a man writing a word
Thought it most completely distils him
Or did not write it —
All of his legend five minutes old moving thru the sixth
The strata under six — eons and eons —

He might type *camions* or *cars*
Instead of scribe as in the fourth minute
Chariots and horse.
The study of history —
The tree, the knee, the tea,
Societally and cyclically —
Sees thru a glass darkly:
Walsinghame;
Waltzing it an era,
Dusty unseen harps,
So rich in determined loss
The loss flames and reacts,
Radiates in words,
The inert less than an eyelet, a flower ray,
The sixth layer is Troy.

Measure, tacit is.
The dead hand shapes
An idea — seeming tiny potential
Musk — a bee robs and fertilizes.
Friends are merely bitter.
And after sixty years of
Incandescent lamps
Glass still flows like honey
Or freezes into the stone of
Striped candy children love —
As such —
True glass
That melts in the mouth
As in the rain —
Their frost-bit noses —
Durable fire.

A what-part invention —

Mildew'd ear, have you eyes?
You cannot call it love,
The hey-day in the blood is tame?
Goodness dies — it happens —
In his own too much,
Holding no quantity
Love looks not with the eyes but with the mind
                                        — is blind.

Voice: first, body —
Speak, of all loves!

You must name his name,
Half his face must be seen thru the lion's neck,
"Ladies, I would entreat you
Not to fear: my life for yours."
One must come in with a bush of thorns and a lantern,
Some twelve years later with Birnam Wood.
Some man or other must present Wall.

Did Bach think sometimes like the Chinese —
Reason: the face of sky?
A Chinese sage speaks Chinese,
But the important thing is
What does he say? He of the *Gurre-Lieder*.

For Centuries
As true as truest horse.

You see an ass-head
Of your own, do you?
This is to make an ass of me,
To fright me if they could.

Do what they can.
I will walk up and down here,
And I will walk up and down here,
And I will sing.
Titania bespeaks these feet:

What angel wakes me
From my flowery bed?
Gentle mortal, sing again.

So is mine eye
Enthrall'd to thy shape —

The weaver's dobbin bobbles:
Methinks, mistress,
You should have little reason for that;
And yet, to say the truth,
Reason and love keep little company together
Now-a-days.
The pity
... some honest neighbors will
Not make them friends.

BOTTOM

Thou art as wise
   as thou art beautiful.

Not so,
But if I had wit
To get out of this wood.

She sings her aire:
Out of this wood

Do not desire to go;
Thou shalt remain here
Whether thou wilt or no.
I am a spirit of
No common rate,
The summer still doth tend
Upon my state,
   I do love thee.

Paracelsus' *Book of Bad and Good Fortune:*
The sun shines upon all of us equally
With its luck. The summer comes
To all of us equally
With its luck. Our love is unequal.

Verbatim:
Good Master Mustardseed, I know your
patience well. That same cowardly, giant-like
ox-beef hath devoured many a gentleman of your
house. I promise you your kindred had made my
eyes water ere now. I desire you more acquaintance,
good Master Mustardseed.

Child first, then ox-beef —
   two thighs in his rump.
Eyes moistened, too.
Groin hit, breaks,
But in building
Persists as vault —

Or my father's story
Of manoeuvres
In Most (mŭst) when he was eleven:

"Bechardi!" "'Morgen!"
"Was machst du?"
"Ich mach ein *outhouse!*
Hoch!"

"So
How does the Czar sleep nights?"
"His regimental lights
Shout his despites
Into artillery sights:
'Shah! Shah! Shah!"

The best man learns of himself
To bring rest to others.

He has perched over — why — valley.
In the pines
He is merry, he's free.
He sleeps, he walks
        his colloquy.
His hut's on the crest
Whose drop has largess,
He sings neighbors are far,
His roof's timbers make sense.
If ridge cloud or rain
The world thunders by,
He awakes: eyes,
A face of sky.

Reject no one

       and
Debase nothing.
This is all-around
Intellect.

The time would be too short —
Throw some part
Of your life after birds —
Eat and drink.
What cry tops older
Fame — far-sighted
Not sure sense? Heart
With mind quick to love,
Look to the real thing
Unfold it within you
Turned there thru pleasure,
Bound anew.
Sweet thing, merry thing
Making your brow
Half an arch of a bridge
So that all people there
Facing round
Quicken their pace,
Fleet and lean
Desire you but to
Thirst what you have —

From Battle of
Discord and Harmony
Come home beloved.

Light lights
Unknown to you

"Glad they were there"
Such happy sorrow
Flying not to
Lose sight of it
Before you found them
In you again
The red-head priest's
Vivaldi's notes
A Jew's maybe
Running from mass,
That fall anew
Our uncommon notes
Our uncommon gold,
Pale gold like halos
Setting off faces:
Who can crib
What time never heard?
"Then he put
His horse into
His pocketbook"
And you can't put
A horse into
A pocketbook
Even an old horse —
Despite what Lorine's tiny neighbor
Told her the night
She was a rich sitter.

You remember
The houses where we were born
The first horse pulsed
Until the evening and the morning
Were the first day?

I'll tell you.
About my *poetics* —

$$\int_{\text{speech}}^{\text{music}}$$

An integral
Lower limit speech
Upper limit music

No?

To excel in humility
Is not to be humble.
Humility does not glaze
Other bodies,
With fellow creatures
Sees agony,
Is the stronger body,
With the eye of sky
Eats food that
Guano dressed.
Not a swallow made that summer.

Time qualifies the fire and spark of it.
I can't improve *that.*
That closed and open sounds saw
      Things,
See somehow everlastingly
Out of the eye of sky.

Poetics.   With constancy.

My father died in the spring.

Half of a fence was built that summer.
For minutes as I drove nails in the lower stringer
The sunset upside down
Tops of trees, even an inverted hill,
Gauze. In the high sun
Paul spoke of garlic-salt as gargle-salt.
Spoke all the time.
C. *would* call the cottage Clostrophobia.
Of clapboard. Without the terra cotta
Of a della Robbia,
A family of three
On *terra* with grass windblown
At first tall in the new cattails.
And so little space —
Three tiny rooms too many —
It had to be shipshape.
Almost on the back cement step
Cattails — hardly *firma*.

My father, where shall I begin?

Who will know what you meant?

To get out of the world alive
Despite despite —
To live among ordinary men
And yet be alone with Him;
To greet profanity
And from it draw the strength to live,
Said the Baalshem —
Thaew —as good as his name.
To sing a michtam of David,
To be alive, that is good.

All summer
Paul babbled of him
Living his life
In young memory.
Ready to speak, like grandpa Paul.
"No let's call the cottage
Grandpa Paul.
I'm sorry he died,
he asked me to come on
a week-day,
when he could buy me a toy
I liked him
better than everyone."

To begin a song:
If you cannot recall,
Forget.

Sabbath, the pious carry no money
Make no purchases.   They have everything
From Friday — the Eve of the Sabbath.
Rest.
A long Sabbath.

His father, my grandfather
Maishe Afroim (the Sephardim speak differently)
Faced East in the synagogue.
Ebon hair?
On the Eve of Sabbath, at the end of Sabbath
At home
So good his singing voice
"Sing bridegroom to bride"
"Sabbath has gone"
Neighbors stopped at his windows

Leaned on the sills.

A voice out of the tabernacle —
For the ark
Shittim wood — the acacia.

The mind that proportioned in stone
Has run from what thorny wood
Tremulous, globular flowers
Yellow, white circlets aflower
Has abstracted from the trunk trimmed
Set up for one day and moving tomorrow

    The Sea ripples in Aphrodite's drapery
    Her peers are the Fates — marble.
    Red stain of her dawn is on them.
    Enter the stone treasury
    From the East, Greek,
    Forget olive grove in a victory:
    Your Virgin is chryselephantine,
    Aegis of Zeus.
    The door out is under,
    The West pediment —
    That broken triangle — standing like you —
    Nearly night upon
    Marbles of Earthshaker and Virgin
    Fighting for order in Athens.

Even Odysseus returned to the sea,
His oar not to be known from a winnow.

Still fighting in northwest Greece
The 8th division

In the Grammos Mts.
Homer described as the gateway to Hades.

The infinite division — love, its wit so divided

No matter —
And from it draw the strength to live —
Refugees and D. P.'s
O. M.'s and M. A.'s
Even Stephen Hero:
"Let him Aristotle" (who fled Athens)
"Examine me if he is able.
Imagine a handsome lady
Saying 'O, excuse me,
My dear Mr. Aristotle.'"

What Philo gained (?) lost to Javan,
About and rejected
So that Jesus after prayed in Gethsemane,
O my Father.

In Hebrew "In the beginning"
Means literally *from the head?*
A source creating
The heaven and the earth
And every plant in the field
Before it was in the earth.
Sweet shapes from a head
Whose thought must live forever —
Be the immortelle —
Before it is thought
A prayer to the East
Before light — the sun later —
To get over even its chaos early.

"You should not forget Him after crossing the sea,
Pinchos"

Maishe Afroim to Pinchos —
Paul, after he had crossed it,
To those who could not say Pinchos.

Naming little Paul for him
Almost ninety —
I knew Pinchos would not mind
Their "English" names being the same.
He might have said to reprove me:
Jews remember the dead in time
Are in no hurry to flatter the living.
He never reproved me.
"Let it be Paul — I know
Ivanovich named for Ivan,
Before he is born.
Still, our Hebrew names are not the same.
Bless him, may he live
120 years."
And the end is the same:
Bach remembers his own name.
Had he asked me to say Kadish
I believe I would have said it for him.
How fathom his will
Who had taught himself to be simple.
Everything should be as simple as it *can* be,
Says Einstein,
But not simpler.

What can make the difficult disposition easier?
Not to be difficult.
Can there be
A difficult composition?

"I'm an artist," said Paul, my son.
"I'll do what I want
The violin in the morning,
a mister of arts,
a red fire in a blue fog at night
in the afternoon paint" (1/13/50)

A Michtam of David,
So many times on his lips:
You have said to Him
My goodness does not extend to you,
The pious in the earth and the excellent
Are all of my delight.
These lines are pleasant to me
That I have inherited.
My heart teaches me at night.
You are before me,
You strengthen my right hand
That my breath rejoices.
You will not let me see death.
You lead me to life
Its pleasures, with your hand
Forever.

My son:
When you teach me —
I don't teach for hire.

To have asked such a man as your grandfather
If one may bite off
Charitable interest
From that or this loan,
Or lick off premium
            from learning

And from whom
Is out of the cave
Of Shag Red or
Air-conditioned *dialektiké* —
A Sum (you say)
Post-mortemer
They should have taught
You more.

Where are my dead breathing friends?
Must one spread his tongue as a doormat
             for a friend to step on?

Good Friday — that's a pun.

Don't learn for revenge,
Question and question, do not be ashamed.
So that all misery may go up into the air with smoke,
As Paracelsus railed
A David in him:
As smoke is driven away, so drive them away.

Schoolmen —
Singers go before,
Players on instruments

        Chenaniah for song
        (Grace) instructed in song
        Because he was skillful

Again, again
Despised
By the pack that is large,

Whose understanding and art are small —
My father, who's never forsaken me
Died and I buried him.
Few are the nights I spend in one bed
As I speed to sick bodies on horse
From the poor I leave behind me:
I gave up a thin body.
All beds are racks.
They'll kill anybody they feign to treat who speaks truth.
Their understanding and art are small:
I think about that in us
That does not die,
I grow leaves.
Don't scorn me
Because I'm alone.
You run off, I am new.
My cure
Steeps in arts
That work out alike:
Alive loves,
Know and don't guess.
In this, wise,
Life's a long
Second paradise.

"My eyes are bloodshy"
(Clear, I see, clear)
Said my son
After practicing
An hour on his fiddle;
Speaking of *Lloyd*
The new boy to play with:
"His name sounded
Very familiar,

But after a while
I got used to it."
Of a dream he dreamed
Paganini playing
Mozart's Turkish Concerto.
— What did he look like, Paul?
— A river!

Like Grandpa Paul.
The water is all of my mind,
I walk the bridge
And the only word I think of is *high*
Man who lives, his speech rattles in throat
                                and head
The sky a tine;
How great the Soul is, Lord Dexter,
Do you not all admire and wonder to
See and behold and hear?
Can you all believe half
The truth and admire to hear —
Illiterate lord of a court of ships figureheads —
How a man *drownded* in the sea
What a great bubble comes up at the top of the water
This is the wind — the bubble's the soul.
All these dead years.
My mother sat away from the stoop,
            the new bridge going up,
To catch her breath in the hottest summer.
Some old landmarks down
The bridge is aging
Effaced their ties
And their sorrow —
History, all its cornices.
Where is, moping?

New York's skyline's a mist of Egypt?
Where, my son, are my dead
                    breathing friends
Effaced in my lines, my growing sun
Who imitates my steps
Whose profile's likeness to me shocks
Who says "My God —
Good gracious"
As the bridge trolley darts
And breathes himself
And understands me best
Because he does not understand.

There is too much air in the air.
Too many stars too high.
A spring mattress pronouncedly spring
This is a "fall to" table, it leans
From New England, not Manhattan.
When I sit down to eat, my father drowses.
This is a "fall to" bench-trestle
It leans to the table.
My guest Henry (masculine)
What a face has the great American novelist
It says: Fie! Nancy, finance.
I have just met him on Rutgers Street, New York
Henry James, Jr.,
Opposite what stood out in my youth
As a frightening
Copy of a Norman church in red brick
Half a square block, if I recall,
Faced with a prospect of fire escapes —
Practically where I was born.
Breathing quite affectively in the mind
Ready to chance the sea of conversation

And unshamefacedly — it has been like a warm
day —
The look of a shaven Chassid,
Were it possible to either him or Chassid,
Takes an impressed step forward
Pleased, not ominous in behalf of the blind or the
publicist —
Said the Chassid:
If you do not, Lord, yet wish to redeem
Israel, at least redeem the Gentiles.

I cannot be too grateful for what you did for Rutgers
Street
(Or for Baltimore, "That cheerful little city of the
dead")
You went down-town once
At that no beard shaking the head

     — Let me go, the dawn is on us
     — No, not until you bless me first
     — Your name?
And the sun rose (chaos to come)
And he halted.
And once before, toward Haran
Lighted upon a certain place
And stayed there, the sun had set.
Stones for pillows.
He dreamed
There were angels going up and down a ladder.
Standing over him a Voice:
— I will give you the land where you sleep on stone,
Seed the dust of the earth.
Blest.   And in you everybody —
       west, east, north, south.

And awoke afraid
— How dreadful is this place
None other but His — the gate to Him.
Said: Keep me in the way I go
With bread,
A coat to put on —
To come back to my father —

In peace
200-year spruce at least
For a fiddle for Paul:
Save
The heart of the wood so to speak
And who belongs to it.
Paul to Paul,
Recall surely,
Carved, not the chips of the process,
Whence are the stems?
He sang sometimes, my son,
When we let him talk,
A chance lilt,
After prayers —
A shred, a repeated word, his whole world —
As, like Bottom,
You might blunder on *tumblesalt*
For *somersault*, Paul.
"They sang this way in deep Russia"
He'd say and carry the notes
Recalling the years
Fly. Where stemmed
The Jew among strangers?
As the hummingbird
Can fly backwards
Also forwards —

How else could it keep going?
Speech moved to sing
To echo the stranger
A tear in an eye
The quick hand wiped off —
Casually:
"I loved to hear them."

As I love:
My poetics.
"Little fish," he grieved
For his wife.
He prayed to the full moon
Over the prow
Alone on that trip
Not seasick.
He returned
For a last look
At Most
After the fire.
His boy wept
And would not let him go.
But he kissed and kissed him and crossed
The Atlantic again alone
This time to
Bring the family over.
What did he not do?
He had kept dogs
Before he rolled logs
On the Niemen.
He swam
Dogpaddle
(Dexter, Paracelsus!)
What a blessing:

He saw Rabbi
Yizchok Elchonon
Walking
On the wharf
In Kovno.
The miracle of his first job
On the lower East Side:
Six years night watchman
In a men's shop
Where by day he pressed pants
Every crease a blade
The irons weighed
At least twenty pounds
But moved both of them
Six days a week
From six in the morning
To nine, sometimes eleven at night,
Or midnight;
Except Fridays
When he left, enough time before sunset
Margolis begrudged.
His own business
My father told Margolis
Is to keep Sabbath.

"Sleep," he prayed
For his dead.
Sabbath.

Moses released the horse
For one day from his harness
So that a man might keep pace.

A shop bench his bed,

He rose rested at four.
Half the free night
Befriended the mice:
Singing Psalms
As they listened.
A day's meal
A slice of bread
And an apple,
The evenings
What matter?
His boots shone.

Gone and out of fashion
His beard you stroked, Paul,
With the Sabbath Prince Albert.
I never saw more beautiful fingers
Used to lift bootstraps.
A beard that won over
A jeering Italian
Who wanted to pluck it —
With the love
His dark brown eyes
Always found in others.
Everybody loves Reb Pinchos
Because he loves everybody,
How many strangers —
He knew so many —
Said that to me
Every Sabbath

He took me —
I was a small boy —
To the birdstore-window to see
The blue-and-yellow Polly
The cardinal, the
Orchard oriole.

Everybody loved Reb Pinchos
Because he loved everybody.
Simple.
You must, myself,
As father of Nicomachus
Say very little
Except: such were his actions.

My life for yours.
Goodness dies —
The humming bird flies forward.
Buried beneath blue sky, bright sunlight.
You'll remember:
The eleventh of April
    1950.
The twelfth —
Snow flurries —
Tasting all unseasonable weather early
Alongside his "little fish"
There 23 years before him.
John Donne in his death-shroud
A saintly face in praying shawl —
He died happy
If you want to know
What he looked like,
Scop,
What are you asking?
He retired on old age pension —
$26 a month —
At 81 — not too late,
He did not covet charity —
Or what has become of it —
And supported his children
Not sure now whether to

Put 91 or 95
On his tombstone.
He had forgotten birthright and birthday,
Who can remember
When every new day
May be turned into account.
What do you await?
If occasion warranted
He could tender his hand to a Polish countess
Playing the glass harmonica
And she wouldn't take offense.
His clasp pocketbook is in a lower drawer
Of his old chiffonier no one wanted.
$3 and some pennies
Saved for the synagogue —
He had hoped for more
But gave away
What he could not spare
To his bungling children —
Praising and showing their photos
They gave him.
The street never wide enough for him,
Taking a diagonal to cross it,
To open and close the synagogue
For over six times ten years
Until three days before he died —
A longer journey than Odysseus'.
Now his namesake says:
"If it's not my kind of words
    I don't want to hear them."
He died certain —
With such the angel of death does not wrestle —
And alone,
Not to let me see death:

"Isn't visiting over?
Go home,
Celia must be anxious,
Kiss Paul."

Measure, tacit is.
Listen to the birds —
And what do the birds sing.
He never saw a movie.
A rich sitter, a broad wake.
Not a sign that he is not here,
Yet a sign, to what side of the window
He sat by, creaks outside.
A speech tapped off music.
Draw off —
Still in the eye of —
          an acacia.
Division: wits so undivided.
A source knows a tree
          still not in the earth
In no hurry to shadow the living
He opens the gates of the synagogue
As time never heard
Lifting up the voice.
Actions things; themselves; doing.

Father to son to grandson.
People carry a wood
To him.
What do the cars
For the horses? Most
   heavenly music.
Summers,
Is it your or my or his hand,

Paul, picks the rambler —
Playing as you do when alone —
Owed the world nothing
Left it with tied
   billets-doux of sons' letters.

A chest weighs at two f - holes of spruce,
On 8½ oz.
That support it:
A fiddle.
Then *it is* Stainer —
Jacob Stainer —
16 hundreds —
In the Austrian Tyrol
Knocking on a tree
Sounding it to make sure
Its wood will be right.
Sitting away from the lumberjacks:
Felling —
Listen to them
Already shapes of violins
Tumbling down the side
Of the mountain.
One of the Stradivarius brothers
At his bench thru 3 sieges
Tells someone quietly: "you wait half a year
                        or go elsewhere,
The wood's not dry for working."
The brothers had
A resin of pine
Since died out.
Then it was Joseph Slavik
Of Chopin's Vienna:
"Excepting Paganini,
I haven't heard

Anything like it — he plays
96 staccato notes
On one stroke of the bow."
You don't want to be the
    fastest player, Paul,
I would like to hear you
Play Old Black Joe
And the Largo
                again
And the red-hair's
        Concerto in A minor.
Pinchos knew nothing about it —
Except the intention
A song fathers:
Bit of red hair
Lost in black,
Gloss of black
In my Paul's gold-red-brown,
Who's ever sure of color?

Rabbi Pinhas:
From true prayers
I took as goodness gave,
The pupil is dark and
Receives every ray of light.

Bread and a coat:
Both are — considering
Our nature — enough with
Which to see the sky.
There, night, and sense sure,
Else not motion or rest.

Rabbi Leib:

What is the worth of their
Expounding the Torah:
All a man's actions
Should make him a Torah —
So to light up
Whether he moves or is still.
Given a share, the body
Comports the soul.
It sees its reflection
Only when it bends to it.
It is not the same
Asking a friend,
The world is its place.
It joins mouth and heart,
The place and its presence
Where each creature sings its song,
It is ruled and acts
First note to fourth,
Because of its holiness
Its song seems not holy at all,
As in the "Section of Praise"
Uniting the degrees:
As it is, created —
And — ashes and ear —
Do you hear yourself,
You must stop.

Rabbi Pinhas: It teaches a man.
There is no one who is not
                    every minute
Taught by his soul.
A disciple: If that is so
Why does it not rule?
Rabbi Pinhas: The soul teaches,

It never repeats.

A word spoken
   in the name of the blest
And blest lips move in the grave
The live lips that speak it
Move with those of the blest.

It is no small thing to
                  hearten men
But the quiet cannot speak
Unless a tie sustain their dead —
That the pure body bear them up
With their light it receives
Pure oil beaten for light,
To glow — not to grovel.

When dust lights up is it even?
And when men count as they have given
Do they not slight what each is?

If it helps, diffract crystals and tracers.
Rabbi S said:
— You can learn from everything.
What man has made
Has also something to teach us.
His chassid jumped:
— Does a train?
— Yes, in a second
One may miss everything.
— A telegraph?
— Every word weighs.
— And the telephone teaches?

— Also. What we say
Here is heard there.

After the Preacher

What shall I teach my son
Who told me Xmas 1949
"There was H- playing
The Turkish Concerto
By Mozart —
Eight records,
And a lollipop
Thinking what it is" —
Or as he paints four pictures
"Around" letters
On different color papers
U — The Rides of Australia
    — on lavender
L — The Woods of Chinese
    — on blue
A — The Chinese Restaurant
    — on gold
PZ — The Sun of Chinese
    — on white —

The economy of force?

A poem whose wisdom seals the seed,
My thoughts to his,
Or facts eye of sky may read?

At a certain age the child cries about
His right to handle a gadget

Or a system for flushing one's water.
As I said one night impatiently to Paul
Who had waked me, and forgetting
I hurried, lèse majesté, to flush
— Crying about flushed p?
Or as compunctious Archibald observed
Between elderly garden chores,
How people
Respond to the curtsy of a European
Kissing a lady's hand —
"O he's a lollipop!"
To which words Paul composes a rondo
A perpetual motion.
Shall I teach Paul my nerves
Are involved in this?

An animal's scratching?
I forgot — the coffee *perking*.
If I remember coffee
Or *Phaedo:*
The lover of wisdom
Does not ask her love
To release her again
To pleasures and pains
To be undone again.
Weaving, instead of unweaving,
A fiddle —
Or Penelope's web.

Shall I teach him:
Who serves the public,
A heavenly singer at a feast.
Or: the noblest embraces the whole art
Involving by no means

The smallest traction of reason.
Or: that cannot be praiseless
Which considers each word.
Or: the lady shall say her mind freely,
Or the blank verse shall halt for't.
Else: What players are they
With flowers of odious savours sweet.

Shall I graph a course,
Say *look at* but let this not take you:

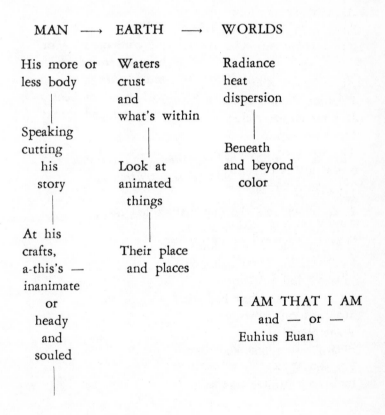

MAN ⟶ EARTH ⟶ WORLDS

His more or
less body

Speaking
cutting
    his
    story

At his
crafts,
a-this's —
inanimate
    or
    heady
    and
    souled

Waters
crust
and
what's within

Look at
animated
    things

Their place
    and places

Radiance
heat
dispersion

Beneath
and beyond
    color

I AM THAT I AM
    and — or —
Euhius Euan

For tenure
  of
"history"
(*his* story)
  and
characters
  and
character
  and
commerce

$$\frac{1 \quad \text{being}}{0 \quad \text{non-being}}$$

SUBSTANCE

being
non-being

Texts: Things
Axiom: He composed — or
        hunted, sowed and
        made things —
        with hand or bent —
        is matter and thinks

Just as if what each of them fights for
          may not be the truth,
Lucretius.
P. Z. remembers the day "Aristotle" died,
Still owns his snowshoes
Indispensable in Macedonia.
I bought him two balloons:
"Plato" and "Aristotle".
Filled with air they had faces
Mounted on snowshoes.
As expected
"Plato" went first and then
"Aristotle" —
Carus, to Paul it was sad.

Dear Spring goes her way with Venus.
Before them —
Inevitable wonders of winds,
After — the west wind,
Flowers run down the lanes.
Next, heat parches
Fullgrown grain blown dusty
In annual gusts of the North.
And it is autumn.
Dancing step by step
With Euhius Euan.
Then Volturnus.
And the south wind
Whose strength is lightning.
Last, snow.
Winter renews numbing frost
Chattering teeth.
Why is it wonderful
That the moon is inevitable?

Like hell of flames
Shooting out of the tops of your heads
While your feet freeze
L. N. wrote me of our winter.

Quire of will
And fated,
Had Shakespeare read him —
Cribbed this?
Since in our body
Riches do not increase
Nor does lineage
Nor kingly pride,
Be sure these are nothing

For the mind.
For all that, the terrors of men
The cares that dog them
Are not awed by arms or by wars,
Trespassing as kings
And lords of the world,
Fearless before glitter of gold
And bright purple,
Come to ruin winning statues
And a name.

Dread of death drives them
They hate their lives and the light
Till their fretted hearts
Contrive their own deaths —
Unaware fear of death drove them
Cankered their honor and friends.
The body shattered by time:
Frame brittle, reason maimed,
Tongue raves, mind stumbles.
Stench final. Sleep may last then
But none thirst what he is.
Nor do diverse songs
Stop flying, wet salt savours
Into the mouth, eyes
Not a wit deceived,
There in the spots light is
And shade, nor do eyes
Know *the nature of things*,
Do not accuse the eyes
Of this fault of the mind.
Can reason sprung from false senses
Speak against them?
Unless they are true
Reason is false.

Can ears judge eyes,
Or touch debate ears,
Or mouth refute touch
Or smell disprove it
Or eyes show it false.
One sense cannot prove
Another false.
There are places out of sight
Filled with voices.
What the mind sees
And the eyes see — the
Shape of their ground, the same.
Dreaming kings storm towns
Cry aloud, murdered,
Without moving.
Love herself is away
Her ways are at hand,
Her name sounds.
Triune of seas, land and sky
A day shall hurl to ruin,
Burden and fabric of the world
Fall headlong.
And the golden morning light reddens
Grass and dew.
A time set in all things.
Age has its teeth fall out
(More gold in his mouth than he is worth)
And the hairless youth
Grows hairy,
A soft down flows
From either cheek.

Shakespeare read somehow —
And whom?

Considering researchists
Should by and large be discomfitted
As one emendator said:
— If a dog hunted fleas
         on mathematical principles
He would never catch a flea
         except by accident.

Shall I teach Paul,
In Shakespeare is *militarist* —
Not recorded again until 1860?

A poetics is informed and informs —
Just *informs* maybe — the rest a risk.
Or: that a bit of culture
Dies a sudden death
Of a man over ninety
That much culture is little breath —
Infinite things in
Infinite modes
Follow divine nature
Being such.
Or: remember, G. S. begins
"Making of Americans"
With a quote
From Nicomachus' father —
With patient father and angry son —
That she said,
"How can you know
More than you do know
And we are still in the shadow
         of explanation,"
Add to her insight ("in all periods before
Things had been said

But never explained.
So then they began to explain")
Long before "before"
Too, they had explained a long time.

Much Shakespeare in Aristotle,
A great deal of Shakespeare
From his young pulse
As he grew older.

Beyond Physics:
All men by nature desire
(It is put — but, in effect, *love*) to know
We delight in our senses
Aside from their usefulness
They are loved for themselves —
And most of all the sense of sight
Brings to light differences
               between things.

Ethics or *Character:*
Seeing seems at any moment complete.
It does not lack anything —
Like coming into being —
To complete it.
Pleasure also takes this form —
At no time more complete
If it lasts longer.
For this reason it is not a movement.
Said Nicomachus' father, in character,
A character sometimes caught up by words
In his teacher's *Republic:*
Eyes, their excellence, that is, sight —

Justice like sight, hearing, health
Or any other real, natural,
Not merely conventional good.
Elsewhere, beyond physics,
He reproved his teacher:
How can we know the objects of sense
Without having the sense,
His Forms destroy the things
For which we are more ardent
Than for Being of the Ideas,
Whatever that is; —
To us, forms effect the arts
For whose sake mind and nature move,
If forms do not move
Where is motion —
Plato wiped out the study of nature.
Rather he wrote on double palimpsest —
On some pages nature is erased
And on others enlivened,
As it were restored.
It wouldn't do at any time
For some Northwest Coast Indian
To re-collect *Be* as an archetype of bees
And neglect his *to not-be* —
A verb which he has —
No more than it would have done for an
                              ancient Hindu.

If love exists, why remember it?

So to light up
Whether one moves or is still.
Number slain.
Hearts remote, yet not asunder

Distance, and no space was seen
Reason, in itself confounded,
Simple were so well compounded —
Is it any wonder
A commentator
Doubts Shakespeare worked these lines?
Their source?
Character, father of Nicomachus —
Simple the certain nature —

Those who sing Psalms,
Odes of bright principle
Come from the sky,
Uniting the degrees.

Appealed Inthehighest.
We speak of heavenly songs.   They
Are intoned neither by harps nor lutes,
Are a noise in the clouds
An echo from earth;
In the stars the skills are arts
All crafts are hidden
All wisdom, all reason
Also all foolishness,
Without Venus, no music would ever be
Without Mars, no crafts
(Planet — not war)
Man was not born of a nothing
But from a substance
Limus terrae — extract of stars
And all elements.
Therefore the Great World
Is closed
So nothing can leave it.

Close to it there is the Little World,
That is to say, man,
Enclosed in his skin
That bounds his body,
And with it he sees
Two Worlds that must not mingle
(As the Sun shines — but itself
Does not pass thru glass —
Divested of all but light —
So the stars light one another inside him)
Earth — seen and touched
Heavens — unseen and untouched:
Together life.
As herder sees each people,
A living mirror of the stars,
Each with its lot — a guide
Never to be copied exactly,
Teaching never to repeat:
The body attracts a heaven
That imprints nothing on us
Endowed as we are with complexions,
Qualities, habits, endowed
As we are with life.
The child's mother is its star and planet
Man is the Little World, but woman the Littlest.
And Great, Little, Littlest has each
Its own way but all three are borne.
One single number should determine our life: 1.
Greater has no peace or rest,
A calculator counts further
Who can say at what number be stops?
This question gnaws Paracelsus.

Better a fiddle than geiger?

With either there is so much in 1
And in one:

$$\int_{-1}^{1} \int_{story}^{sound} \quad - \quad eyes:\ thing\ thought$$

Who can adjudge stages
Or write wisely
Where cycles started or ended,
Without stories to drag them —
Men's actions encompass whaletooth to scrimshaw?
The town Mystic has as it were a toy drawbridge
    on Main Street, wharves, ships;
Its marine museum speaks red and black India ink
    where sail needle pricked ivory, speaks
Of file, pocket-knife, wood-ashes, sailors' idle palms
                                        scrimshanting
In 1820ies.   "All these 24 hours
Small breezes, thick foggy weather."
The brig *By Chance* made no sale.
"So ends this day, all hands employed scrimshanting."
Polishing.
Not mystic: sand and sun
By water.
New waterfront street recobbled with old cobbles
New to this water.
Courses tide, and a tide
                brings back folk
                after twenty years,
A cycle a light matter or more,
So my song with an old voice is whole:
Another way of saying
You cannot take out of the circle — what was in it,

          that is and will be —
A father "patient" and "angry" by turns
        as his son sees it
Either another event
Pinprick of contents, but an assemblage
     of all possible positions —
The locus, sometimes —
     As Baruch said accursed, nevermind blest —
     Since men would rather imagine than understand
     And chance is imperfect knowledge
     And body exists as we feel it
     And essence is that remove, that degree,
       without which a thing is no thing
    (Defined is defined)
     And nothing happens in the body
     That is not perceived by the mind
     The mind also conceives by its power —
A contents that is as in the song "sweet content."
     Since no one cares about anything he does not love
     And love is pleasure that dwells on its cause
     He who loves keeps what he loves:
     An image inwreathed with many things
     That may flourish, that draws cause
     To light up.
     If the understanding perceives the idea of
                    quantity as cause
     It determines the quantity
     So to speak from motion
     (A line from motion of a point,
     A body from motion of a plane)
     Yet these are not understood
     Unless quantity is perceived
     And the motion be made to endure
     Forever,

Which could not be
Without a thought
Of infinite quantity.

"The horse bends down" — Paul, '46, May.
A center as it were
From which his hoofs
Spark clusters of stars
That weaving bobble
No one spark the same like another —
But there are families of them
It becomes involved,
Sometimes arbitrary.
The horse sees he is repeating
All known cultures
And suspects repeating
Others unknown to him,
Maybe he had better not
Think of himself
Hunting so to speak
Sowing so to speak
Composing always.
The shape of his ground seems to have been
A constant for all dead horses
His neigh cultural constant
Also his sniff —
It is some such constant when a culture
Seems to revert a hundred years
Or some thousands?
And instances from "different" cultures, surprisingly
                                        inwreathed,
Seem to look back at one another,
Aristotle at Shakespeare (both so fond of blind heroes)
And blest Spinoza at Shakespeare —

How?
Or for that matter uninwreathed
As Rig-Veda at me,
Because none has to read the
    other yet it happens.
As Bach calls to composers and writers of my time.
If Paul loves Bach I need not tell him
Johann Seb Bach, as he calls him,
Is present
His legs in a *gigue*
   Old French, *to dance* (*giguer*) or *hop*
From *gigue* (Teuton *geige* — a fiddle)
Half his seat out of his seat at the organ,
Like his contemporary hopping Chassid
Who might have shook
To the Prelude of the Third Partita.
In someone else it's Theocritus
Supposed to come thru
Does he know it.
One's a lucky horse
For Bach's jigging fire to come thru
And be new.
Take that of Lear, my friend, who has the power
To seal the accuser's lips in behalf of
Some with insight, some with a great deal:
Bottom W., Polonius T.,
Hamlet H. (for Hamlet) Adams —
Or what composer is it modal from M. Croche
    not a bit (not a bit modish?) too soon —
Believe I am Seti First
    presenting Lotus to Osiris: it
Hurries to Socrates
Whose words are real
Otherwise why must two words balance opposites —

To Socrates nature does not walk on one leg only.
Has then nature legs —
Countless? A poet dares beg the question;
Hemlock Socrates purging a scruple
Bothered before death — he had never before
                                    bothered —
    to try the sound of words,
Turning, after loving wisdom, Aesop to rhyme.
Just as the eye that sticks with rime cannot move
When faced to the wall of a cavern from
Darkness to light
            without turning the whole body
So the instrument of knowledge
Plays only when the beloved's head
Turns from Passing to Being
So learns by degrees —
Who knows what Plato thought anyway
With so much sight honeybee, to sound
How perilously. "The eyes of the mind are proofs,"
Spinoza, did not mean to be Plato, how could he?
What is this Sight of Being?
Plato: "its brightest and best — good."
Baruch not dupe to think it was made for man:
"A man can neither be nor be conceived
        without the power of enjoying the greatest good."

Sane, vain and mad enough
To call himself Paracelsus:
In each (of Three Worlds) an urge to exceed
And none wants to act with measure,
To the end that balance be
And no crooked thing,
That nothing exceed the circle.
Rests before the mirror

Where its image rests. The image
Is not sole object of knowledge. Nor is man
Whose knowledge comes from outside him —
The mirrored image he is.
Together men form one sky.
The sky is a man,
You must know this to understand
Why places are different
And things new and old
Why everywhere things are different,
You cannot find out
By looking at skies alone
But from their effects.
One sky is rich in each of us,
Undivided.
When a child is conceived
It gets a sky for a gift.
Fire warms thru the walls of a stove
A man's body acts from afar and rests,
Qualified by the forces that flow from it
Its thought is abroad,
Neither that of element nor star,
Free for new craft to flow into it,
All arts are not in one's country
But everywhere in the world
There to be gathered and sought.
The physician learns from old women,
Gypsies, peasants, vagabonds
People at random.
Art pursues no one, is rather pursued,
But everyone wants to fly before he has wings.
(Some hundred years later the blest:
A timid child thinks he can fight.)
Medicinal roots are in the just heart

Each part is judged from the work
This art puts wisdom to work
By wisdom art makes it,
Despite there is poison in all things
The dose makes it poison or not.
The physician's schools are three —
Elements, stars, the Light
All burn in him.
And tho he is earth —

The horse — between his hoofs
And ground sparks rise
The four hoofs of each horse
Are different, different from his fellow's horse
And the ground is worn —
Wears the light of nature —
(Nothing but reason — love —)
There it is, yet what is gone is gone
And it is the new Time.
The horse plods and learns
Neither sleep nor Sabbath can rest him
If he is called on to write a book
And it is put by for a life
Nothing fails it
Cared for in his mind,
He need not rush at the book.
It is never late
What must be born.
At last he finds
What he has never
Learned or seen:
Man a shape like
The satyrion root,

Chicory high
When the sun is in the sky
Its root a bird
After seven years.
If you know the answer
Keep still,
If you don't, try
Find out.
The carpenter's beam runs thru his head
His virtue forms *his* shape.
Who draws maps pores over
Hands of landscapes, countries, streams.
Old son and — or — new,
Whiling away
Is not whole.
To plod is not hobble.
Each time has Love's way with music.
You keep up to date
On all fours
That canter sometimes
Before boughs that grace trees.
Sparks from hoofs:
There is horse;
Like-sparks
His old love or new reason
Expect.

So year to year —
Nor do the arts
Ever end.
How can man say
"I am certain"
For certain and uncertain

Do not make certain.
Only forever is previous
And not a horse's forever.
If someone stole off with its body
Be sure that its spirits
Canter forever.
Blacksmith, creator, shapes his shoe
Into substance.
What is rot?
Take elderberry's
Man sees in winter
He hardly knows it the fool,
Shivering beggar —
The pope will likely desert him —
But if it's his hum he carries
He tastes his desire.
Nothing is ever finished,
Complete.   True
No animal lasts after death.
Wisdom's enemy is no one
But unwise,
Liar —

Wise stars can be led
        by his foolish.
He who knows nothing
Loves nothing
Who does nothing
Understands nothing.
Who understands
Loves and sees,
Believes what he knows,
The horse has large eyes
Man's virtue his feeling.
His heart treasures his tongue, certain

That a *yes* means no *no*,
What else is happiness
False storekeepers, false traders,
                    false brothers?
(The body's exists as we feel it.)
What is unhappiness?
Against — against nature.
Light is not unhappy.
Night: not unhappy.
Who walks in both, or in either, walks well.
Who does not fall is ordered: more horse.
Who falls is disordered: no horse.
Uncountable stars
Can one ever approximate all of them.
— Don't estimate for me
Read what it says, asked Paul.
I was trying to abstract
A story
From the Levitical sacrifices.

For all inwreathed in me
That make my love
Your fiddle,
To some imagined music,
When it shall be your own
In the world, thru some sense of the bow
                                    alone
Shall tell the strings
Their Great World quietly —
In the time I owe the world nothing —
    What in you
Of my father who owed a Source
    Or his little fish
Of when I walked with him,

With you or with Celia, a night
Or with the winds
Say what their wonders with cities are
With seas in arms of landscape, a thought or a hand
Slowing that I do not see death
When an air seems too much in the air:
My time will run me
I am not all of my time
No one is all of it.
M. Croche wondered about Alessandro Scarlatti's
Writing at least 106 operas:
Good heavens how gifted the man must have been
And how could he find time to live,
There's a *Passion according to St. John* by him
Whose choruses seemed to be written in pale gold
Like halos, primitive frescoes (M. Croche Antidilettante,
Asked nearly the year
I was born near the Third Ave. "L"
Where we lived looking into a dance-hall) I cannot
imagine

How he found time to have a son
And make a harpsichordist of him —
Domenico.
My time runs me
With primitives'
Divine arabesque:
Ornament not in
Musical grammar.
Palestrina, Vittoria, Orlando di Lasso
Strengthened its delicate traceries --
The bass of their form —
By strong counterpoint.
When Bach renewed arabesque
He made it more pliant, more fluid.

What stirs is
          his tracing a particular line,
Tracings of lines
Meeting by chance or design.
With him *ornament*,
  acquires
A precision of appeal —
Let no one think it
Unnatural.
As Spinoza said in this line —
If they understood *things*
My arguments would convince them,
Simple mathematics,
Altho they might not attract them:
There cannot be too much merriment,
It is always good.
To make use of things, to take
Delight as much as possible
(Satiety forsakes them)
Is the part of a wise man,
To feed himself
Good food and drink,
To take pleasure
With growing plants, dress, music,
Cities which men may use without hurt
          to their fellows:
The human body has parts
          of different nature
That continuously want new
          and varied nourishment
So it may be apt to do
As can follow from its nature
And the mind at the same time
Understand many things.

This manner of living
Agrees best with our principles,
Wherefore, if there be any other,
This manner is best,
In all ways to be commended,
Nor is there need
To be clearer:
The human body needs many bodies
To be, so to speak, regenerated,
The human mind can move other bodies
                    in many ways

And dispose them in many ways,
It is apt to perceive many things
And more so according as its body
Can be disposed in more ways.
A sound akin to mosaic:
A rhythm of eyes
Almost along a line
Looking into and out of the frame —
Empress Theodora and court ladies
Moved to the East
Where the sun begins.
Unearthed catacombs
Brought into the sun
Whereto is playing
A good shepherd's song
Amidst plenty of sheep.
Saul struck: "Whose son?"
"David, the son of" —
            his psalm.
Intervals only of seconds,
But not harping all over the stave,
Fingers imperceptibly moving near
Strings ready to sound

From open to stop in a twinkling,

Disposed in many ways
No less surprising and quiet
Than that, 1313, Rabbi Hacen Ben Salomo —
(Great One Singer Son of Peace) —
Taught Spanish Christians
To dance in a church.
No less surprising and quiet —
To Ambrosio and Guglielmo, Jews
Said to dance "above all human measure"
    a special license
     from the Pope (1575).
Guglielmo's pupil as good as he
Jewish minstrels and troubadours
By that Sea literally in the Middle of Land,
Dances and cities which men may use
Without hurt to their fellows
With justice flamed with freedom
What more happy song than one's lot?
Love does not wish you to be anything else.

As eyes one does not work to dim
But rests so they work a whole life — the future
No lighter for greed of it —
Their need seeks no death
In extra chores that close them with pennies,
People are pigs,
Precisely, pigs are not people.

A poet is not at all surprised by science.
That you may play better
Paul, who saw "Beauty and the Beast"

And asked how soon will the beast become lovely,
For all inwreathed
This imagined music
Traces the particular line
Of lines meeting
    by chance or design

Well, now then,
With the winds
Says what their wonders with cities are,
With seas in arms of landscape,
This music
Moved by a thought to a hand —

In my city one wished me death,
Nevermind,
The stars last more than one night —
    The hidden so disposes imagination,
    And so the body to take on a nature
    Opposed it seems to itself, of which no idea
    Can be given the mind, but that a man
    Out of need of his nature should try not to exist
    Or appear changed
    Is as impossible
    As for any thing to be made out of nothing,
    This everyone with a little reflection
    May see:
    Anyone can kill himself, compelled by some other
    Who twists his right hand
    Which holds perhaps a sword
    So it is led against his own heart,
    Or like Seneca by the command of a tyrant,
    Be forced to open his veins,
    To avoid more evil by taking on less —

Many things sleepwalkers do
They would not dare if awake —

All of which shows
That the body can do many things
By the laws of its nature
At which the mind is amazed;
No one knows how
The mind moves the body
(Cerebral charges? were discovered
Some time ago thru poetry
Not surprised in the least
By new science)
Or by what means,
Nor how many degrees of motion
It can give the body,
Nor with what speed it can move it.
Whence if men say this or that action
Arises from the mind
That has power over the body
They confess specious words
That do not regard it with wonder;
When the body sleeps
The mind's unconscious (Spinoza very early on
                                                that)
Has not the power
It has when awake.
The mind is not always apt
For thinking its subject,
Only as the body is apt
For the image of this or that
To excite it
Does the mind see the object.

I looked

When we dream that we speak
We think we speak
From free decision of the mind;
Yet we do not speak, or if we do,
This decision thought to be free
Is imagination — or memory;
Is nothing but the accord
An idea involves.
A suspension of judgment
Apprehends, is not free.
In dreams also we dream that we dream,
I grant no one is deceived
In so far as he perceives.
The imaginations of the mind
                              in themselves
Involve no error,
But I deny that a man
                    affirms nothing
In so far as he perceives —

                              SPINOZA.

Facing south, I looked
At the ferry at South Ferry
At night, the ruins of Castle Garden
Where Jenny Lind sang
Before my time — with the diamonds
Of the songs of the nightingale —
Long after the Castle became the Aquarium:
Swung back by my young pulse,
Recalled a seal in teal blue,
A compass in binnacle —
Asleep or sleepless
Held on to Paul's hand.

The full moon rose.   Flowed in the water.
                                    The harbor
Had the sea's face: C's face as expected.
And unknowing, Haran
Lighted south, west, north, east
The red ferry pulling out of its slip
Its bell ringing
By intermittences
Our bloods submitted,
Like crazed Randolph
Ringing a bell sometimes in Congress
Was it? and muttering "it's all over,"
The New Jersey farmer's
Improved wagon-wheel
T. J. uncovered in Homer
And the first John Jacob Astor's
Landing in Baltimore
With $25, and seven flutes to sell —
So much change.
And it occurred to me
How cities rise and fall,
As once in Cambridge,
During the last war
When Scollay Square tap danced so lively
It rose as it were Queen Elizabeth's heir
In Boston: there on SECRET business
(Everybody's the next day
Tho this anybody worded no breath to —
How a war gets around!)
But the eyes more congenial
To the Xmas candy building
        of Massachusetts Hall —
Some time to think over a day away from home —
Before going back to the hotel —

Looked — before '76
When Boston breathed cannon —
Old North Church is lost at the foot of the hill
Boston is an old copper sink
    its freighted harbor viewed from Mather's grave —
Its story: North Station to Back Bay to Commonwealth
The same in New York,
Lower East Side to Village to Riverside Drive.
Slums where the first had settled by water,
Rich founders moved inland
Leaving a silt of poor,
Insolvent wealth spooned into an art colony
With some Ciceronian virtu earning
The rich estates furthest up the river —
The silt burnished to catch up,
As the city rose and fell, everything "too much"
As Fred Allen chid "for the Moses model human body"
The greatest networks, THE most executive
Carbon monoxide, noise and bubble gum yet,
All eyes, not one, Fred Rockbottom,
Equal to one flyspeck,
From soap to razors
Everything extraordinary
Washed clean and black as a nobleman's
                      posterior —
Go and praise London, waltzed Chopin
Whom his lady friend was used to seeing in heaven,
In this angel's case
Being alive or dead
Did not matter —
The attraction that led instinct to pursue
                so many and
Such varied lines to such great distances
Intensely strong and indefinitely lasting

The quality that developed   the eye and the wing
                of the bee and the condor,
To support friend Hamlet Adams again,
Is not in suburban mixture
Starting anew in Westchester
After it is all over with the Bronx.
The kings that were:
General Blacksmith Work — Welders
Bell and Kilhaullen
Coliseum (that was)
Starlight Pool (that was)
   Rink
Worth Knowing McSorley's
Cabinet Makers (that were)
A ship's figurehead,
Used Cars
Atlas Baby Carriages
Wise Motorists Simonize
Post No Bills
Stop Dead End.
I asked then
Where are the coppers of New England's
                first business men?
Not in Gloucester that does not fish for the air
                of Brittany.
The Nantucket Whaling Club
Is run by selectmen.
And I asked again before the New Battery Tunnel
Of my image of Archie
The most graceful trunk
I had ever seen more or less
Between Easter and Halloween
Reading me a Chopin holograph, over a drink:
        I correct the Paris edition of Bach

Not only the engravers' errors
But those listed by those
Who supposedly understand him,
I do not claim to understand him better
But I am convinced
That sometimes I can divine him
Archie ended,
— I am not always at peace in my mind,
You have missed the salvation of a
          Glorious sunset. It
          Is too late now.
Beaming. And it was night.
The railroads brought in what's around town
And died out —
The point they made of arriving was to start out
                                        again.

So I listened
To them hail me: a friend —
Where are your fathers?
And do the prophets live for ever?
A friend, a Z the 3rd letter of his (the first
                    of my) last name,
Pursued by Zechariah maybe —
Age leads to reminiscence
    as he might say:
— Of making many books
So much a day jotted down
In a notebook assures them.
There's the other extreme
Who makes his life a notebook.
— We all do. Much study wearies.
Let us hear the conclusion,
Or, *read the conclusion then*
That Koheleth, Celia, read "Pericles."

— Have you been writing lately?
    — Ivy twines bare beds.
        Alone, sing two:
        Two brothers:
        One.
        Magnolia and dogwood,
        Spring's Xmas froth
        Sing two:
        2 brothers:
        One.
        The ivy winters green.
        Stark ivy twines, green alone.
        Each brother knows
        Stone befriends its own.
        Stones know each brother alone,
        Each that the other has none.
        And gay, gay
        Magnolia and dogwood
        Spring —
        Sister

In a non-Jewish, non-Gentile world
Singing of Chanukah and Xmacy brothers
Who send gifts once a year
Every family apart,
He shall bring forth
The headstone crying
Grace, grace to it,
Change of raiment
Nations be joined
    Be my people,
Not by might —
    By my Spirit.
Who despised the day of small things?
See the plummet in his hand,

the Seven-branched candlestick:
Eyes run to and fro
Thru the whole earth
And two olive trees to either side
Burn light of themselves.
(When I have
Raised up thy sons, O Zion,
Against thy sons, O Greece?)
That ten men shall take
Hold of all languages of the nations
Even him that is a Jew
Saying, We will go with you?
The curse over the face of the whole earth:
Their likeness thru all the earth.
(TV? "The screen is," rocked Chidbottom,
"A problem.

How can you show a glint in somebody's eye.
                        Small minds, small talents
                        Hide in a flea's navel
                        With enough room
                        For the heart of a network.")

— Six nights on one page,
No complaint,
Only in the end to write it
Exactly as sketched
      in the first draft.

— It is as it had to be
Or tried to be
Light not clear nor dark
Not day nor night
At evening it shall be light.
Words commanded the prophets
Did they not take hold
Of your fathers?

They returned and said
According to our ways
Our doings
He dealt with us.
Should I weep in May
Separating myself
As I have done so many years?
Guile helped forward the affliction,
Fearing: old men and old women
                For very age
Streets of the city full
Of boys and girls playing,

A painter's thoughts
Of children singing without notes
As they eyed each other,
His wager on a genius
(A blur to a renowned violinist)
Singers and poets
Wild elegance and conciseness,
The works that become all hours
The hour they no longer hear
Save the excellent —
In Delacroix' sight
Sketching horses,
Of his trade longest to learn
That asks the learning of the composer,
The occasions of the violinist —
Works that practiced
Strengthen twisted fingers
And that the unpracticed should not attempt
Before seeing a surgeon,
The bodies for whom without Bach
The fingers are not free.
To memorize, that love make the tone.

This science of Mozart
Wreathing all instruments
So that timbre understands timbre
And each moves to all
Not to fear

Wonder ...
Said the impalpable-palpable novelist —
Which fortune may deal on occasion
Those whose faculty
For (pious?) application
Is all and only
In their imagination
                           and sensibility.

Never fearing one
Who sees faster
Into a generalization
Than his knowledge of details
Extends, said his brother,
Laying a plane under all formulas
And enmities, where men
Meet, not paid to talk.
I grow sick hearing myself
Unable to stop.
False words helped the affliction.
But worse
That men out
Of the need of their nature
Should try not to exist
By blowing up ruins
Of the Warsaw ghetto,
Not beasts, a terror
Howling "Sub-humans!"
To have pursued the
Tortured in the ship *Exodus*

To DDT DP's
Scuttle their prison ship
With a justice that does not exist
In the world but sterilizes,
To become stiff as boards
With no chance of ever being thawed out
To lie with frozen snow-spattered
Horses for nothing
Icicles two inches long
Hanging from spectacles
In front of dead eyes,
Not fear to look
Like death warmed over,
To wolf crumbs
From a flying roll
Eat raw cabbages
Whole
Nothing human in common
After being lashed in common.
— Whoever speaks
Is ready
To help forward the affliction.
— It is not always easy
To separate. myself
When I look
At my son's hand,
For all actions
Which passions determine
Are determined better
By a reason like love.
To raise the arm
Clench the fist,
Bring it down
With the force

Of the arm
Is a good joined
To an image of hate,
And desolate, is
Not love, it is blind.
We may see why desire
Roused by a passion
Is called blind by us.
Things that bear harmony —
— Did you sing
        prisoners
A song that may
Snarl you today
— That bear harmony,
The form of a song,
                    equity,

Reflect no *yes*
That means *no*
If it sang then
It still sings.
No prison
No false dealing
Can wipe out the tone
Sounding a time.
Can love rouse a thing of the past
And not see it as present?
It is not easy
To exceed the circle
One's hand in it.
Fish that fly out of the ocean
Flying fish
            go back to it.
The song does not think
To say therefore I am,

Has no wit so forked.
Between the simple
And *therefore*
Is a chasm.
Only our thought
Says, our cave
Was not simple
Dark once — a false leap,
That our clear art
Moved to diversity
Understands and
Depicts our lives better.
Hope says this
With cave in us sometimes
And art in others
With art in us sometimes
And cave in others —
As thought, extended,
As body, minded
With countless effects of
The same infinite
Not infinite
As affected by
One of us
Actual as he is
But only in so far
As it is affected
By another
As actual
And still another
And so on
To infinity —
This is history
— You say

You speak and sing
And that you dread
The abstraction?
— The song in the head?
Why should I dread
What outlasts
Snarled hope,
Is more than
Where no one is,
There where anyone is.
To those who flee battle
And those who hurry to battle,
Say love your hurt reason.
Lasheyes, says Paul
Meaning eyelashes —
But the language of
Diplomacy is such
I am never able
To verify it.
Shall we look at
Those who fear the uranium in the earth
Will be gone
Before man
Is exterminated,
Those who
At a command
Over the radio
At zero minus one minute
Fall prone on the ground
Eyes fixed there
The head away
From zero
Saying I'm sure
That at the end of the world

In the last milli-second
The last man will see what we saw,
Who shudder that peace might break,
Who will eat for the lack of red soil
His limestone remains.
Too windy and chilly for energy.
Look at that soldier, I said,
  Guarding the dock,
As fast and as poised and as cold
As The Discus Thrower.
Dead alive. Ideal.
The white plaster cast
Of that day of athletics. Military, not merry.
'Murder can be comic,'
Charles Chaplin had to explain,
'The logical extension of business,
As to Von Clausewitz
War was the logical extension of diplomacy.'
Olympian "observer" who models after an Ideal
In stone is himself a discus thrower,
Athlete with anatomical belly
In love with his own genre body —
Paradoxically *transcendental.*
Said the blest, such terms
Arise from the fact
That the limited body
Can form in itself
Only a certain number of images,
If more are formed
The images begin to be confused,
If exceeded, they become entirely confused.
The mind then imagines
Without any distinction,
        under one attribute —

A universal —
Man, not
The small differences,
And predicates concerning an infinite number
                              of individuals.
Like chitchatty women who never conceived.
The author of *Great Expectations* saw no one here
Getting anywhere without a rocking chair,
As today sees the poor farmer with two cars
A few steps from the A&P —
Not a Pompeian who relished fruit
     even in stone lintel,
Hears Delegate Thunder suggest to reporters
Shelled Jerusalem might be saved by an
                              appeal to the Godless.

And wonder, can the man
Who said —

               What did we gain by a pact?
               Peace for a year and a half
               And the opportunity of
               Preparing
               Despite the pact (1941)

     And:

               May God help him
               (Roosevelt) in his task (1941)
     (And was made Chief Fallen Trees
     of the Mohawk Nation that year
     and told Mr. Wilkie — That's a very
     good phrase, I certainly try to
     keep my eye on the ball (1942))
     And: The German wolf is not bad
               Because he is gray
               But because he ate the sheep (1944)
     And: I drink to the health

                    Of the people
                Considered cogs
                    In the wheels
                Of the great State apparatus
                But without whom all of us —
                Marshals and army commanders
                Are not worth a tinker's dam (1945)
    And: I do not know whether
                Mr. Churchill &
                            (At Teheran, Churchill presented
                                    the Marshal,
                                        shoe cobbler's son,
                            for the citizens of Stalingrad
                            a 2-handed sword from King George.
                            The Marshal kissed it)
                Will succeed in organizing
                A new military expedition
                Against Eastern Europe,
                One man says
                They will be beaten
                As they were 26 years ago (1946)
    And: Things are not bad in the U. S. (1947)
    And: Warlords guided
                And didn't understand anything
                            about the economy (1947)
    And: Language serves all classes
                In a society equally (1950)
Can the man who said all these things
Answer all questions
In ambassadorial memoirs
And not have read
Mao's best-man poem:
                Drawn by mountain and river
                Many heroes submitted.

Pitiable Emperor of Ching
   and Emperor Wu Ti of Han
Not wise enough.

So, too, Emperor Tai Tsung
   of Tang and Emperor Kao Tsu
   of Sung.

Genghis Khan strung only a bow
And shot arrows at vultures.
Gone.

To make sure of heroes
We must wait and look into
       our time.

Military and Ideal:
The end of the known world —
That the ambassador and the "leader"
Each in his representations for his people
Must be secret.
Paul's sense of the present is clearer.
— Does Lars come from Troy
Where all those men fell?
(He had misheard:
Troy for *Detroit*.)
Flaherty took it hard,
Called down for not
Making clear the social burden
Of the Aran Islanders
And tried to explain:
The burden of the horizon
Can be as heavy as any,
Its burden filmed thru the
Eyes of a child
Wailing, let me go!
Pablo the Ur-realist
Faced by his "Guernica"

And the Gestapo officer's hiss
"Did you do this!"
Said gently, you did.
Of the Igorots
Hoisted on top of tanks
To serve as the eyes
Of American drivers,
Said MacArthur:
Gentlemen — When you
Tell that story stand in tribute
To those gallant Igorots.
Of whom Gracie Allen —
"If he's not careful" —
The burden of the horizon
In the Altai Mountains
Of Siberia
During the last war
Under fifty feet of ice
A Russian scientist
Chopped thru, he
Uncovered a log stable
Bronze Age axes
And the well-preserved bodies
Of 10 horses
Saddled and bridled.
Where the round of sky
Awakes the eyelid
And where people gather
The world takes hold —
After being with them
We brush cobwebs aside
Even after hearing crickets
Enter our rooms
Chivvied by swarms of insects

And ask is it wrong
To tell our enemy
To give up his arms?
Wrong for him
To ask us?
If what rolls between
My eyelashes
Could receive all of the world
I should indeed
Be struck blind.
But: if a man's honest
Even *once* in his life,
He should be counted.
I don't care about
Power, but this care of *once*
After all is said
Gives me some eternity.
We live by presuming
Infinite nose —
No spoor is lost.
So record
Politics,

    Record
Labor.
— Marx's presumption?
— He wrote fugues
On a theme of Aristotle
    — His footnotes corroborate —
That boiled down simply,
From his body to other bodies
There's a natural use
And a use that's unnatural.

I'm talking you to sleep, my friend?

Consider the man
On the West Coast
Who read *Das Kapital*
For 25 years
Who when the law
Ordered the Communists
To profess,
Came into the open;
For all that
The FBI
Found no Party card
With his name
Or a pseudonym —
He had not understood
The law, the Party
Had in fact
Turned down an application
For membership.
— That's what's funny
About the law.
If the legal mind's worth more
Than a tinker's dam
Its interpretations grow powerless.
You remind me:
On one of my long walks
Out of Los Angeles
A dog followed my chaps,
For miles.
Maybe their oil-smell
Attracted him;
Four-lane highways
Did not stop him —
A mixed breed —
I couldn't shoo him off.

I walked faster
Trying to keep a distance
Between us,
So the motorists
Wouldn't blame me for him.
I wouldn't touch him
When he caught up.
So he'd run ahead
And look back to make sure
I was following,
And wag his tail.
I couldn't hide from him
So I thought I'd better
Get off the highways,
And when I slowed up to cross
He was hit. But not hurt.
We stalled the traffic
Northbound and southbound.
Then I could not
Resist
Patting him.
Dope, I said,
Why did you do it?
You must be hungry
I'll feed you.
What's good for a dog
I asked at the diner.
"Hamburgers."
I ordered two huge ones
Well-done,
Do you know
When he saw them
He ran as tho
They were poison.

I never met
That dog again.

— Reincarnated?
An old friend, maybe
Free to run off
In his other life
Refusing
Obligations
That come
From being fed?
Shall we have some coffee?
Dutch, if you insist.

I will hiss for them
And gather them;
For I have redeemed them:
They shall increase
As they have increased

— Sheridan sat
In a tavern watching
Drury Lane that he had built
Blaze away —
Making almost a verse:
"May not a gentleman
Take a glass of wine
By his own fireside?

Consume, consume it
With its timbers
And its stones

I was dreaming

I couldn't see.

Nothing.

When we dream that we speak
We think that we speak

Look, I said, Paul, Bowling Green
Is the same as when
I played George Washington
With a toy sword
That cost 10¢
Knee pants skimpy —
The bridge going up —
And took turns
Also acting both
Wolfe and Montcalm
All to myself —
The Baroque building
That curves with Broadway
Across from
The Customs House
Still standing,
All the streets
From the Battery to 14th
Filled as they were
All those from 14th
To 23rd the same
And Metropolitan Life's tower

— What's Orient Life?

The ships named
For kings and queens

Go out of the
World

So
Akhnaton
Moved
From his stomach
Towards the sun
Day and night

Fishy-wishy
Washy-whittle
Little soul
Hadrian's
Hailing itself,
What will
Become of you,
Roman?

Abroad
As the four
Winds
Of the heaven

Spread

A sleep
Coming on
As over Odysseus
And Penelope
Both
Before
Great

Archery

Almost seeing
Thru the sounds
        brewing
— Things happen, Paul,
        the strangest things,
You know who that
Pete Fanelli is
We saw yesterday
I, after twenty years —
He worked with
Victor the barber
Whom I used to
See unfailingly
Every two weeks
Because he
Didn't cut hair
He sculptured it

As the sea
The "Artemis"
A slender tree,
At her girdle

I will engrave
The graving
Thereof
In winds,
With seas,
In arms of landscape

— You've got to be careful in woods

If you're not careful, said Paul
Of tree swinging back,
You may on the path,
Going under it,

He might have continued
Omitting some articles
Except that he was
Getting around to

— Slip gerplump
On a stump.

I slipped.
He laughed: You were born to smoke cigarettes.
Wait till they find out
Where you took most of "your" poetry.
A letter, he said.
— Mine, give it to me.
— What does it say?

      Dear L. N.
          So your mother's dead. Today's
such a cool blue day the kind that
follows what we have all of life to
think about — — — Each writer writes
one long work whose beat he cannot
entirely be aware of. Recurrences
follow him, crib and drink from a
well that's his cadence — after
he's gone. What struck you, as
I think you meant, choppy in
"A", 13 years or so back when
I tried hard for the "fact", I

reread sometimes to tie in with
what goes on now, and the "fact"
is not so hard-set as a paradigm.
I have to reread several times
to find out what I meant. Only
after a while, with no pen in hand,
does the "fact" I wanted come
back — a sort of perennial-annual.
What else can you tell me? I wish
you would so I may know.

Like the sea fishing
Constantly fishing
       Its own waters.

The continuity —
Its pulse.

Already a little ode:
How I had to ford
To Hungerford,
I can't afford
Another word.

So no man
Lifted up his head

For hell we launched
And trimmed the gear despite our tears.
The wind came aft.
We sat, steered, nothing to do.
Then the dark: a deep river — alien

To our world —
       where the

Camp Cooke, Calif.
January 27, 1951
12:00 P. T.

Dear Mr. Zukofsky,

Well the way it look know, is that I won't be home for a long time. We finist our basics training last week and now started our unite training. It is suppose to last 13 weeks. After that we will be ready for combat.

I don't know just what is up. Some of the guys say that we will be going to Germany and some say to Korea. But there's a job to be done. I just hope I can do my part. The way I feel is that I would rather be back home again. But I guess that's the way everybody think. I just hope by the time Paul grow up he won't be in it. Tommy has to register the end of this month. I guess they well let him finesh high school.

Well I guess this is all for now. Hope everything is OK. back in New York. Tell Paul I was asking for him.

As Ever
       Jackie

UNITED STATES ARMY

Dear Mr. & Mrs. Zukofsky,

There isn't to much new here. We still are working hard. There was a rumor the first of the month that we all were going to leave, but we are still here. They did take out 20 guy. From what I understand they are going to Koria. I guess I was lucky. But it's just a matter of time I guess before we all will be leaving.

I have K. P. tommrow and I an trying to get all my letter writing done today. So please excuse my writing.

I am taking a couple USAFI courses in Plumbing. I don't know if it will help me, but I will now a little more. There are quite a few guy taking these courses. If I make out with the first course I am going to try to see if I can get a high school deploma. Thank you for the cookies you sent me. I got them the other day they were very good. It make me feel good knowing that somebody else is thing of me. I got a letter from Peter and he said that it was snowing back home. I guess it's pretty cold back home too. The weather is pretty good now. The temperature go up to about 80 during the day, but it get pretty cold at night. And right now I have a little cold.

Tell Paul, that I am all right and if God is willan I will see him someday. Tell him, that we salute the flag the same way we salute the officers except when we are under armes then there are different ways of saluting.

As Ever

Jackie

Paul:
— With snowman falling down.
The sun disappeared with snow.

Delightful happiness with the snow.
With the sending of pictures to L.
Two little flowers —
Still more —
All the trees have turned red.

— where the Cimmerii live:
In cloud and fog no sun ever
Broke, or a star.   Beached in pitch-dark;

Camp Fuchinobe, Japan
April 27, 1951

Hello Zukofsky

I don't know just what to say. So many thing
have happen in the last month, that I can't keep up
with then. But I will start when we left camp. It was
Friday, March 31, at 9 o'clock at night that we left.
We aboarded a train at the camp, that took us to San
Francisco. We arrived there around 8 o'clock Saturday
morning. At 10 o'clock we aboarded the Breckinridge.
The ship that took us to Japan. There was 2,700 GI.
on it. After being on it for a week we cross the 180th.
Merdian, commonly known as the International Dateline.
Of couse we were all initiated into the Royal Order
of the Dragon-backs.   You can guess what happen.
Most of the guy lost all or most of there hair. I
happen to be one of the first to go through and didn't
lose much. I didn't get sea sick as I though I would.
The first day out I felt kind of funny, but after that
I was alright.   I think if I ever have to go into the
service again, I will go into the Navy.   The boys on
our ship had it pretty easy.

Friday, April 13, we derk at the port of Yokohama 5,263 miles from San Francisco. We derk about 1 o'clock in the afternoon and stay on the ship until midnight. (What for I don't now) After getting off the ship we had to wait for two hour untill our train came. It took us another two hours to get to the camp, wish is only 25 miles from Yokohama. So you can see how the railroad are in Japan. The only mean of transportation are bicycle, trains, and your feet, which they used quite abit. The shack are nothing but paper. I wouldn't want to live here all my life. The only thing I can say is "Thank God Ian an America" You don't realize how well off you are until you see how they live here.

The cost of living is very high around here, a haircut cost you 25¢. At the snack bar you can get a hamburger for 10¢. It's just like being home before the war. For entertainment on Sunday we go sightseeing and shopping tours, Monday they put on a show, Tuesday they have Japanese entertainment, Wednesday is bingo, Thursday they have a dance, Friday we have more Japanese entertainment, Saturday they have another dance, or you can play pool or ping pong. For other entertainment there is a bowling allay, theater, swimming pool, tennis court, baseball diamond, and the one everybody will attend when they get pay, the beer hall.

We are suppose to get paid this coming Monday. It just so happan that it's the first of May, and we are on the alert. From what I understand the Communists had a big time here last year, so they put us on the alert this year. All the guy are hoping that they do do something, so they can get a little exercise. You see this camp is only one mile square, and it only hole a battalion, which I am in. There is no place to train, so since we got here, we haven't done a thing. From what I understand we will be leaving this camp the 8 or 9 of next month. We are suppose to go somewhere up in the mountain to finish our training. We are all hoping that when we finish our training that we come back here. Then we would have it made. But then again the Army doesn't work that way. The day we left the camp the mail man came up to me and ask me if I wanted the job. So what could I say, but yes. The job isn't to bad. One reason I took it was that I didn't have to pull KP. or Guard Duty.

Well Mr Zukofsky, I don't know of anything more I can say. It look like I ran out of word. Tell Paul I was asking for him and hope he is alright. I hope you folks are to.

As Ever
Jackie

Camp McNair, Japan
June 14, 1951

Dear Zukofsky,

Ian very sorry I didn't write before this. But Ian so far behind in writing to everyone, that it isn't funny. Please for give me.

Well there isn't to much to say. We stay at Camp Fuchinobe for a month and then we went by truck to Camp McNair. When we were at Fuchinobe why, I went into Yokohama. It was quite a ride You have to change trains about six times. It was very interesting. You should see the thing they have for sale. I think everyone in this county know how to paint. There are three or four guy around here every week painting pictures. And they do a good job.

On the way to Camp McNair the land look beautiful. The first big hill we went over we could see Mount Fuji and didn't it look beautiful. It took us five hour to get to the camp. When we got there, there was a sign at the gate which said in Japanses. (This is hell) You can believe that. You couldn't walk anywhere with out getting all mad. It isn't to bad now, I guess we got here after it had rain for a couple of day. The Camp is right at the base of Mount Fuji. I think the mountain has something to do with the weather.

Well I guess it won't be long before you will be going to — —. I hope you have a nice summer there. Tell Paul I was asking about him. Well I guess this is it for now. Hope every thing is alright. I haven't gone to Tokyo yet. But if there is anything else you want let me know. Be good.

A Poor Pay *Pfc*.

followed
The shore to wet hell

Camp McNair, Japan
July 1, 1951

Dear Zukofsky
I received you letter last night and you glad to here from you. It must be nice to get out of the city. Ian glad that dad got somebody to do the work for

you.

Ian still company mail clerk as of now. No telling what could happen. We got alot of replacement in last week. So now I have to make a report on all of then. Beside that, this is the week we get pay and I'll be quite busey.

I'll tell you, just send me anything. I could use some 616 film. You can't get any here. But there is one little you could send me if you want, and that is a discharge. Ha, ha, ha.

Well I guess this is it for now. I hope every thing is alright. Tell Paul I was asking for him. Be good.

A Poor Pay Pfc.
As Ever
Jackie

AMERICAN RED CROSS

Dear Zukofsky,

I sorry I didn't write before this but with moving and then the first of the month comning up so soon I didn't have much time.

I want to thank you for the candy you sent me. I got it just when I needed it. The food lately hasn't been to good but I guess that the way the Army feed.

Right now we are on a ship heading down the coast of Japan. We are to make a landing tomorrow morning. The way it look now the war will be over pretty soon. I hope so!

Tell me how is Paul doing this summer. I suppose he is alway playing with Peter. If you should see Peter one of these day ask him how the Red Sox are doing.

You better have a bat with you when you ask him.

Well I guess this is it for now. I hope everyone is well.

As Ever

Jack

Jackie, American, Poor Pay Pfc, Roman Catholic
Eyes azure
First seen in marsh thru cattails —
Surprised when I addressed him as Mister.
Trust and honor.
And paid our respects in hell:
Forgetting none,
Praying over and over
Vowing that home —
Crowds from below,

G. S. as an old woman spoke to GI's:
(— It is natural to speak of one's roof
Between four walls, under a roof,
And here was a whole city
Spread without a roof)
You will be flattered to death,
    to death
Because
You will have to fight again.
    (*One of them*)
— After all we are on top.
— Is there any spot on earth
More dangerous than on top?
And there it all was.
South Ferry almost erased
By the wind in the slip.

Horse ran there.
Desire.

Pig-snout belch,
      Sea,
If a lamb
Achieves status of tragedy
As scapegoat,
Why not a swine?

— What does it say, asked Paul.
— You can read, can't you?
— Are you angry?
I don't want you to be —

Speak, if you hear

The hidden so disposes imagination
Has not the power it has when awake —
We or Russia, Iran,
China, India, Israel,
Or all together
Will have let it ride
      with the tide.
The next war setting
A bad baked cake in this.
Ache of an old aunt
Who hurt all over.
Things sleepwalkers do.
   A bastard in Ashdod
   Feeble shall be as David
   That day,
   Angel
  Four trombones and the organ

in the nave
Will quire after six thousand years
The enbalmed tongue
Tip unseen at the lips
Tasting glyph:
Who beat us to it?
Two women
Wind in their wings
Love no false oath.
Easy to distract —
Thought cannot will to hold on to
                         a hand
Nor the assailed hand remember straight,
So easily driven on all hands
The mind is not free to remember or forget
Anything the opened hand feels.
The body cannot determine
The mind to think
Nor the mind the body
To persist in motion or rest
Or any other state
If there be any other.
Friendless
Talked with me
Truth and peace.
Sun shines upon all equally
— A musician's surface, said Paul.
Site at eyes,
Sings an aire
With heart led to it, bespeaks
Horsehair and strings —
Luck equal, a height in the clouds.
The simple is uncompounded
        or well compounded,

Then what the mind sees
     the eyes see;
If the seeds bear,
Like-perceptions shape, love the breathed air.

A man with a tape measure —
Nay, you must name his name:
The latest lives again, a
Child,
Once the circle is closed
It becomes very small
     and very great,
A chance word
  another song
    of
  endless song,
Fern — fruit dot — sorus,
         Sora.

Touched a wall of washed
Stones by the dock
Where a wood sang once.
Midsummer's thorns and a lantern,
A dancing lamp at night on a face
         buried history.
Wind carried larch to ridge.
Patience.
Truest horse.

— it says —
May I read your letter?
"crib and drink from
a well that's his
cadence — after he's

gone ... What else
can you tell me?
... so I may know."
A voiced look gone
— It means, Paul,
If a man sees a thing
      when alone
He goes right away
To look for someone
To show it
So he may hear
More and more of it.
— You see, that's why
I don't want any of us
    to sleep late.

  (Knavery)

When I was angry I
Knew a green leaf
About to fade,
Like Kaikobad —

When you were three
I gave you your coat —
    A serious jest —
And told you to go
If you could not live
  with us quietly.
You shed tears
Of Zal before the Simurgh:
Are you tired of me
Don't want me
In your house

Anymore?

So with his hand
Touched
The "Tick-Tack Uhr"
Midsummer's dream
A night's munificence
That Iran
Had brought Germany.

— Look, Paul, where
The sawhorses of "A" - 7
Have brought me.

In the eighth month
In the second year of Darius
I saw by night —

Thru running manes of Leaves of Grass
In their first printer's shop,
The house it was in still stands
On Cranberry Street
That I walk nights
I go to teach
In the Eagle building, of old
Brooklyn, freighted with the lost
Years and winds of Whitman's editorials —
The mind acts certain
Things and suffers others
Acts before it explains why
Often centuries before

A red horse
Among myrtle,

Behind him
Red horses,
Speckled, and white

— O my lord
What are these

— They walk
To and fro
Thru the earth —
We have
Walked
To and fro
And the earth
Is quiet,
Be quiet, flesh
Isn't this
A brand
Plucked out
Of the fire?
Clothe,
Have
Places to
Walk,
Bring forth
My servant
The BRANCH,
See the stone
Laid —
On a stone
Seven eyes —
Call each man
Under the vine
And under the fig.

Talked with me,
Waked me.
I saw
The first chariot,
Red horses —
The second,
Black —
The third,
White —
The fourth,
Grizzled and bay.
— What are these?
— The black go
North,
The white
After,
The grizzled
South.
The bay
Go on
Thru the earth.

Crying to me,
— See
These go north
And quiet me.
When
  the eyes
   have seen
To everyone grass in the field
My staff, even Beauty
Shall say, I am no prophet.
  HOLINESS

Upon the bells of horses
   In that day

— Look, Paul, the small arrowroot
Has rabbit ears.

— Why?

High   inthehighest
I was unhappy — I've forgotten it.

The fire roared, quieted to light.

Blest
Infinite things
So many
Which confuse imagination
Thru its weakness,
To the ear
Noises.
Or harmony
Delights
Men to madness —
To say the planets
Whirl and make harmony —
That they take for things
Modifications of
Imagination:

Where before,
If all things passed
From the world
Time and space

Were left,
They would now
Disappear
With the things —

It's pleasant
And understandable
That all but a fiddler
Have said "enough."

The mind turns to the body
As object:
A mode that occupies
Is actual and nothing else.
There then
Are simple bodies
Marked out mutually
As moving or still
Swift or slow.

No one
So far
Knows
What a body
Can do
Or can make
It
Of texture
Or
Tick-tack uhr —

From a body's nature
From nature

Under whatever
Attribute
Follow
Infinite things:

Thought
Not image
Or word,

Tongues
That fail quiet,
Desires
That may order,

And what
Men desire
With such love
Nothing can
Remove
From their minds.

None then is free,
We say
With Ovid —
He's iron
Who picks up
What another
Lover
Forsakes.

Hate
When loved
Becomes

Love,
But it's true
No one
Wants
To be sick
To get well.
The way
Things are,
Quiet
Is happier
Than most words.

Let the caustic
Say, "Ass,"
The theologian
Rail,
And the sorry
Praise the rude
Barbarous
Life,
Despise men,
Admire brutes —
If men see
Common ground
How much better
To regard them
Than brutes.

The idea
Is not
In the mind
That can cut off
Our bodies.
To perceive a winged horse

Affirms wings on a horse,
They stay
Unless another idea
With the body as object
Removes wings from a horse
From the reason.

When men count
They do not err
In their minds.
No one desires
To be blest —
To act well
Or live well —
Who will
Not desire
To exist.

This is virtue
The more so
All have it.

Repentance
Twice unhappy,
Pitiable,
Pitiful

But for
The wish
To show
A hurt
Has not yet
Rotted,

That lovers
Bear not
From the misjudged
And the misjudging
Mind alone,
But a marriage
Of things to
                    peace.

Ardent
            good
Nicomachus, the physician, had a son
Aristotle who had a son Nicomachus —
Aristotle's sun? Without him no Mean
Golden or safe wrapped or rapped in the loquacious?
He'd heard Wisdom say foolish things and caught
Its sense, grew plants, fled lest Athens swim twice
Against philosophy from vague feeling
To a bad heart, from wish-bone to no sense —
Lectured walking. Spoke for himself to his son?
We pardon more easily natural desires —
Anger rather than bad taste. Take for instance,
The man who defended striking his father —
Saying, My father also struck his father,
Grandfather his father — and pointed to
His child — And he'll strike me as soon as he
Grows up, it runs in the family. Or
The man who dragged on the floor by his son
Asked him to stop at the door for he himself
Had dragged his father that far and no more.
When love laughs that carefully it has eyes
And Authority has a nose of wax.

The lover of myth loves wisdom: both wonder.
Tents pick up, hoplites charge, Horae dispose.
The wise man lacking detail *knows* at that
And while we must begin with what is known
Things are known in two ways, some to us, some
We say, are known without qualification:
So a certain nature is simple and
Loved, all other things moved to it are moved,
So art that has cannot have more or less,
   As a house loves the ground, is like the man
   Who owns it, it is itself and is his,
   Has a floor and warms, no cellar to flood,
   No attic to stifle the air it breathes,
   It does not leave off making space,
   Its building is an agreeable habit.
Making friends from self-probing, quite lonely
Until we know love is loyal to one person,
Happiness is not present at the start
Like a piece of property and is only
Accidentally concerned with the good
Of the artist –– failing he must blame himself ––
He wants impossible liveforever
While justice is to persons as well as to things.
Nothing is better for being eternal
Or more white than white that dies of a day.
To be is better than not to be.   To
Live —

Celia.

     Over coffee.

The lover of wisdom

Does not ask her love
To release her again
To pleasures and pains.
Weaving,
A fiddle.

Evenings
Or after midnight
Our own and the world's
Recurrences
The untrammeled
Breath one cannot
Wish to stop.
I do not say this to you
Yet you hear me.
Our restlessness is for what things — any
We are and are not — that rule us.
We are as you have said
Lucky.
For you I need not write this
Or write anything,
My time runs me
When I write only for you
Whatever
Is around me.
Literature, you remark
Is in a way another's account
Which if I can afford to carry
May add up as my own.
What culture there is, I chime in, is light
From a persistent fire twitching
Reflections of our momentary flames.
My poetics has old ochre in it
On walls of a civilized cave,

Eyes trapped in time, hears foam over horses,
All of a style, surge
Over six thousand years
Not one of their mouths worrying a bit.
Today no bit to worry.
Paul's "Robin" is in the white frame —
Red crayon redder than the red paper it is on.
Today he insists it is "A Ship"
Not a robin —
A caravel whose high poop
Was the robin's breast.
Three hours away
In the country
Our American blue block-print
On white-duck curtains
Of ships and Seminoles
Hang at the windows,
Recut
So often for the windows
Of different places we have lived in
Cut and pieced once for a bed
Cut and the spare
Pieces laid aside
To be used again,
We begin early
And go on with a theme
Hanging and draping
The same texture.
On the third floor
Of our Brooklyn brownstone
Is my fetish for building,
A collage:
"Duncan Phyfe's house, workshop and store" —
After an old engraving —

Is the lower half of the picture;
Above, right, a postcard
Of Chardin's *House of Cards*
In colors
As suspended as the original,
To its left a doodling
On a scrap of white paper
The lower half pasted
Opposite the high gable
Of Phyfe's house;
From its attic window
Leans a little man
Intended to look maybe from brick wall
Towards sky
Looking maybe — if I've managed —
Out of the engraving,
Up, into a black space
Between the Chardin and the doodling —
Both building like the Phyfe buildings under —
Where Paul and other children
Crowding their answers
On their question
As to what is this scribbling
Have seen a sea of boats
Repeating spars and the like
But not four words
In small scrawl
"So's your old man,"
Not my writing.
The rest I heard I did
Over a coffee
In a diner
After midnight
Thinking to the preludio

of the Third Partita.
The little man
Looking maybe into black
    construction paper
On which all three parts
    of this collage are pasted
And that extends its $\frac{1}{4}$-inch border
To a wood frame.
The whole preserved under a glass
About the size of a sheet
Of manuscript paper:
A realizable desire
Of a genius
In the branch of a tree,
A thought the same as the bough.
"Completely," said Paul
"The sun all thru
December."

A valentine for our genius
Celia —
No false pride —
Merely our tutelary spirit:

    The world had better be thrifty
    I am approaching fifty
    And how many years more than thirty
    Are you — almost forty?

    Not for a haughty mask
    Not in dirty hands
    Not with shifty eyes
    We are nearly

Forty
And fifty.

The kid is proof of that.
You tell him of the Thinkfast School
— Better fast if it's thinking at all,
Three marigolds last thru fall
Dwarf autumn marigolds
Around the sunset of one petunia in the garden —
How thin you look,
No one says,
You've been suffering from poetry
Again, Li Po.

The house is almost warm.
Let us begin with the alchemist and his Little World.
You say such lovely things

       — Whole days fritter away in solitude
       With water as the running base.

The water private bee, says Ovid —
Cleaning: the deep knee bend —
And *as when a conduite pipe is crackt.*
There must be some honor in puzzles and philately,
Working with Paul
Inasmuch as there is rest.
The phone rings

       — A legitimate exchange of ignorance

It rings again

       — That was Mr. Fine
       Telling me how fine he is.

P. Z. is reading about Ben Franklin
Who foresaw a chutists invasion.

> — It was such a muggy day
> The carpenter was ready to paint.
> The laundry man said
> He heard over TV
> A layer of cold air
> From Canada
> Was rolling our way.
> I felt like asking
> Were they going to show it.

I am he that meets the year — Ovid —
A song —
An interest in remaining alive
Who more than Paul's titles
For drawings in this vein

> Suddenly A Fire
> Oil blacks
> Long Without You
> O Pad Fire
> Putting Out The Fires In The Old Days
> Some Posts Have Been Going Down
> Steps Going Up The Apartment House
> West East In The Old Days
> Paul Lying Down Scribbling
> A Harpsichord
> Long Long Ago When It Was Raining
> When Bach Lived

You

— Two tables for the price of none

Notes:
Interest —
An exchange
Of two
  birds' notes.

You were pleased
When the Reverend
Left his notebook
As you noticed
The spelling:
Merditations.

All that follows you here
You may see as
  my object
And your record.

Notes of things
That may please you

Rocks and robbers,
Said Byron's valet of Greece.

    I clear my desk of clippings

Madam Geschwind
At the marine spitoon

    Files and head
    Of twenty years notes
    To make life easier to
      handle

Ibsen scrimped
On postage

Enough for a book

Whatever happens we have got
The Maxim gun and they have not

Must I work on them

Passed by for what better
Few words,
Nodding to others,
And so unlittered
Of impingements

Not worth saving

Changeful persons sought us
Is explanation all that
Friends want

As trace
Of my object

> A sege of herons
> A spring of teals
> A bevy of quails
> A gaggle of geese
> A covert of coots
> A congregation of plovers
> A wisp of snipe
> A covey of partridges
> A fall of woodcocks
> A murmuration of starlings

A charm of goldfinches
A watch of nightingales
An exaltation of larks

The author's purpose is to paint and set before
  our eyes
The lyvely image of the thought that in our
  stomaches ryse.
And yet that does not convey all of a feast of birds,
Tho it may the spell of the poet's *broken ribbes of*
  ships upon the shore:

What now avayles
My Spinoza I take so often
    to the country,
Falling apart, becoming
A descant on the Shakespeare —
Both extolled Ovid
  "The Poet."

A poet is never idle,
My one reader
Who types me,
But I *am* one of your chores.
  Poe to his printer:
  You receive all
  the profits
  and allow me
  twenty copies
  for friends.

On the reverse
Of this sheet
Paul's first cursive

owing account to myself alone
of my hours

Lines — a child's crying face
Smile leading tears to a light.
Of age what wine
To search out their order
Such they may say
Set tears in place —

River, since a song does not turn back
to speak to
Everyone of its order, but will run on
In the words after the sun on
The singer stops shining

Discarded with other tries:

this
and all after death
to kiss
it.

Since the past is a wall
between two windows
one who does not lean out
no longer sees

A redness mixed with white

But if no one be there to present *wall,*
Of these same flowers to please her boy my sister
gathered some
And I had thought to do so too for I was
thither cum

Notes:
Roger Bacon's *Six Causes of Teaching Ignorance:*
Unsound Authority
The Over-Academic
Lack of Willingness to say *I do not know*
Saying *I know*
Pretense to Wisdom
Fear of, and Catering to the Crowd.

"Adversaries have
called me a constructor,
an engineer, an architect,
a mathematician —
not to flatter me —
knowing my *Verklaerte Nacht*
and *Gurre-Lieder*,
tho some people
like these works because
of their emotionality;
called my music dry
and denied me spontaneity,
pretended that I offered the
products of a brain, not of
a heart.
I have often wondered
why (Beethoven) called himself
brain-owner, when the
possession of a brain
spells a danger to
the naivete of an artist
for many pseudo-historians?"

It is honest history to admit *this possession*

And not fatal
Except to the conceit
             of the dull corpus.
Honest to remember that Bartok of another mind,
Like Schönberg, did not acquiesce quietly
That is, stay with his day's Germans.

Nor that other naif —
No clock in his room, but
One at every point in space.
What speed has sound? Why
I don't know. I don't weigh down
My memory with facts I can find in a text.

— Protean but constant, said the Italian
We are a nation of 90 millions.
— But the population of Italy is 45 million?
— Si, si, 45 million that remember Muss
             and 45 million that don't.

The camera
Shows the reaction
Of a hand to a burning
Cigarette, 26/100
Of a second passes
Before it is pulled
Away

The last and highest triumph of history would, to his
mind, be the bringing of Russia into the Atlantic
combine, and the just and fair allotment of
the whole world among the regulated activities of
the universe. At the rate of unification since

1840, this end should be possible within another
sixty years; and, in foresight of that point, Adams
could already finish — provisionally — his
chart of international unity; but, for the moment
(1903) the gravest doubts and ignorance
covered the whole field.

And nothing may compare with years in swiftness
of their pace

Notes:
To me quite moving

Klee, I guess, 1924:
His *objects* of *line*, *tone*, *color*
Equal the *special character* of their *style* —
Said before, of course,
And has been said later,
But for me as by a friend
Who's constant, it goes on —
Now the artist places
More value on the powers
That form
Than the final forms —
On the power-house of all time and space,
Call it brain or heart
Which drives every function.
(Stringed an Egyptian necklace.)

(Sam Butler) he did not see that the education
cost the children far more than it cost him,
inasmuch as it cost them the power of earning
their living easily

For all that untrained eyes

Have missed Weston's joy
Of finding things
Already composed:
After the first print has been made
The thrill's over —
That reveals as it
Makes the portrait
Or portrays the rock

I don't seem to read books any more
Tho I suppose actually
I read them all the time.
I don't read the newspapers
Tho once a week I seem to spend a day on them —
As I did today —
You ask
— What's in this envelop?

These are some things I wanted
To get into a poem,
Some unfinished work
I may never finish,
Some that will never be used anywhere
You don't have to type —
That'll be nice
You won't have to type —
Much of it in pencil — blurred — other
                notes written over it
I can't read back thru the years —
Is it worth jotting down
In ink, as sometime
I may be sorry
When the sense is entirely destroyed.

Perhaps an unwarranted loneliness
          prompts me to it
For not much in it interests me now
If it can't be turned into poetry.

This does not belong with these —
Could have gone into *A Test of Poetry* —
Written when Shakespeare was twenty or so
By one John Soowthern or Soothern —
A poor, I think, text
A bit arranged by me:
> It is after our deaths, a thing manifest,
> We both go to hell, and suffer hellish pains,
> You, for your rigor, I, for my thoughts haultaines,
> That attempt to love a Goddess so Celest.
> But as for me I shall be little afflicted,
> Tis you (my warrior) that must have the torment:
> For I but in seeing you am content.
> You, with me, I'll bless the place so much detested
> And my soul that is raved with your fair eyes,
> In the midst of hell, will establish a skies'
> Making my bright day in the eternal night.
> And when all the damned else are in annoy
> I'll smile in that glory seeing you my joy,
> And being once there go not out of your sight.

Notes for different plays
I'd have done in my twenties
At the slightest encouragement —
Since I suppose worked out
By the legitimate stage.
> A girl says, "Are you sick,
> Why aren't you eating
> This terribly delicious chow mein?"

Her courtly Chinese friend
As he watches
Her American appetite
Drinks tea from a cup
The restaurateur has reserved.
"In it's the scent," he says
"That no washing retains —
No, I'm all right."

For another play: an inner stage for film,
  A book stalks the proscenium,
  Elevators hum in the wings,
  Greek chorus
  Rides Toonerville trolley.

Another: antedating our true-life Italian film.
  A boy of four,
  Manhattan 40 years ago,
  Felicia, a young mother
  Among other poor characters
  When metal sinks had pumps,
  Three flights of stairs down to
  A sort of barracks of johns.

Lights Festival: a musicale
  (Legs of chorus watering
  a cardboard of evening skyscrapers.)

The Windows: the drama of a textile plant —
  workers betting on corpses — action opposite
  a bookstore, in part a chapel.
A theatre that for atmosphere
Smells like water at the bottom of
A swimming pool
(Too expensive to produce?)
Lines for a play?
How tell her
On a night after such lightness

He held her reflection without
An envelop. (That is all I make of it,
                              Celia.)
A setting, with pencil sketch,
Refuse pipes tower above roofs,
Queensboro Bridge lighted above a row of
Low blacked out riverfront houses.

Two operas:
The Ghost Dance (Wovoka),
Ovid's *Metamorphoses*
That would sing Golding.

A historical drama: *Edward VIII*
(The radio addresses of Edward and George,
Kent, Edward cheated of Marina?)
Curiously no Briton has handled it,
How far have we moved from drama
        and Shakespeare's Cranmer:
            "Good grows with her
            Our children's children
            Shall see this, and bless heaven."

A spy story: *The Lifesaver Antenna.*
He rolled the thing which seemed
nothing more than a steering wheel
removed forcibly from an automobile.
The device in it had revealed
intelligence to the enemy.

Two novels:
    The Little Girl: Her presence, 12, was destroying
    whatever friendship I had left for her father. She

paid court to me as his enemy. *Fleur, lys, baume* —
the effect on her of his singing for me these words
of Machault might well have been "bombs". She inter-
rupted, reading aloud as it were her lesson: "In the
twilight of the eleventh inning as Slaughter crosses
the plate an extraordinary crowd of 34,000 went wild
and cushions came sailing from every section onto the
field or among spectators in lower-sections. The
cushion-throwing continued for ten minutes despite
frantic appeals over the public address system."

That People the Sunbeams:
Pace: a "Western," William S. Hart's *Tumbleweeds.*
Frontiersmen and a European family.
The design: a drive of the nature of things
appearing in succession as ground, motion, and a
manifold perception of the former; as over an
abstract plane a shrug saving existence.
Hangars of piers, airy, caged, parallel,
while an eardrum holds quiet. A man's eyes
rests sometimes where a wall meets a floor,
or he stops in the sphere of a thought.
Suddenly a chair is handed across a room,
other rooms remembered by the bottles in
them, wires spring, a bridge fills, a
height would seem to move perceptibly.
Levels sway with handicraft for travel.
A struggle is a dense point, a black spot
where lips might tighten, then a shriek
from a flat screen. A hand senses as never
before the telephone receiver, a body
similarly what it means upstairs. Many
twigs front a look. As to the thighs,
it's the moon, its quarter, if the dress

is not a *lettre de cachet*. The dress
should have nothing to do with it. So
many cultures lost and it is the earth
which is irrigated. A clothesline drips
on the chair in the garden and a sprinkler
bathes in the country for a town its
produce. She looks around, whatever
strain relieved at the sides of her head,
allowing her to see him as they precede
arm in arm gay motes that people the
sunbeams.

Stories: *It Was* — "the country of Watteau."
　　　Rutgers St. (near Cherry St.,
　　　Geo. Washington's days) Two
　　　past-marriageable girls, their
　　　shop, ships, whistles, the bridge,
　　　old mother, America the gilt
　　　country, basement, Friday's
　　　candlestick, pier mirror.

　　　The Hounds: Colebrook furnace, 17c.
　　　an early iron master, a despot
　　　over his community and his dogs.

A Life of William Byrd

About Some Americans: "more Colden," Clarence
　　　　　　　　　　　　　　　　　　　King,
Judge B. Stallo; J. K. Ingalls (*Work and Wealth*, 1878
also *Social Wealth*, 1885, That I have been unable
'to complete the science of economics' should not
be a matter of surprise, since no true science is

ever completed. Natural capital — the land and the
labor. There is in nature no other source of
increase); *How Jefferson Used Words; A History of
American Design; Graph: Of Culture*

Anybody's welcome to it.
Take: a raft of stuff.

"there always along by the side these dramaturgic
life-histories and underlying them, an obscure
system of generalizations in terms of matter-of-
fact (obscure only in so far as it is less pic-
turesque")

Veblen — or Vico:
An age of gods, alien to abstraction, buried in
matter
An age of heroes, the divine in tatters
An age of men, tongues practical and scientific

My idea
        the pyramid contains
                the seed
                the dead King
                the star
                        drawn to its apex.

Why bother more. Give some thought to a performance
Of your *Pericles*, Celia.
P. Z. at 2½
Keeping time with a strand of chicken bone.
To begin a song
If it is not there
Forget.

As *The Changes* sing,
The men of Phrygia built
The walls of Troy
And were refused wages.

Why write an essay
Saying Bach took from the folk
Their church for a calculus,
And Mozart from the folk
Their stage for his calculus,
And some of us
Folk as we are from
Two wars what calculus.

Everyone
Will explain to us
How to do
The wrong things
The right way

I've finished 12 "books,"
So to speak,
Of 24 —

A kind of childlike
Play this division
Into 24,
Enough perhaps for
12 books in this one
All done in a summer
After a gathering of 12 summers.

Aristarchus didn't
Punctuate Homer,
But Gerhardi we read young

"worked for Sir Hugo (of Vladivostok fame)
a lover of staff work ... besides many
ordinary files he had some special files ...
or he would write a report ... once ...
a very exhaustive report on the local
situation ... after much thought inserted
a number of additional commas, read it
through once again solely from the point
of view of punctuation, most particular
about full stops, commas and semicolons ...
very fond of colons — by way of being more
pointed and incisive, by way of proving
that the universe was one chain of causes
and effects"

Item for *A Test of Poetry*,
Elizabeth's *Princess of Espinoy*

Sonnet

When the warrior Phoebus goeth to make his
round
With a painful course to tow her Hemisphere
A dark shadow, a great horror, and a fear,
In I know not what clouds environ the ground.
And even so for Pinoy, that fair virtuous Lady,
Although Jupiter have in this orison
Made a star of her in the Adrian crown,
Mourns; dolour and grief accompany our body.
O Atropos, thou has done a work perverst
And as a bird that hath lost both young and nest
About the place where it was makes many a turn.
Even so doth Cupid, that infant god of amor,
Fly about the tomb where she lies all in dolour,

Weeping for her lies, wherein he may sojourn.

a queen in Bucks County
pulls on her glove to show her gold ring,
tomorrow, tomorrow the wedding will begin

— Still awake, still pothering?
— What, goddess?

— This is your house,
Your wife's here
And your boy.

water, water, white flower growing up so high
white white flower she

— So long as sleep comes in the night, Penelope said.

A thunder from the warehouses
Storying produce

Ancient thunder at the mill
Millstones grinding
Barley and wheat
The marrow of men's bodies.

Thinking's the lowest rung
No one'll believe I feel this.
We talk so late
Let us go to sleep.

When Paul tunes his fiddle
The piano needs tuning
He says "I was right,
The note was right

As I played it the first time,"
You say "his ear
Is better than mine" —
That is love.

Living, you love
So I love
With the dead
In me
Thru wet and dry
For the living

— Tell me

— Tell *you*

Tell me of that man who got around
He knew men and cities
His heart riled
As he strove for himself and friends
He did not save them.
Tell us about it, my Light,
Start where you please.

It's so simple,
Telemachos rose from his bed
And dressed

Blest
Ardent
Celia
     unhurt and
Happy.

(continues)

CONTENTS